THE RETURN OF THE GODS

JONATHAN CAHN

FRONT LINE

Most Charisma Media products are available at special quantity discounts for bulk purchase for sales promotions, premiums, fund-raising, and educational needs. For details, call us at (407) 333-0600 or visit our website at www.charismamedia.com.

THE RETURN OF THE GODS by Jonathan Cahn
Published by FrontLine, an imprint of Charisma Media
600 Rinehart Road, Lake Mary, Florida 32746

Unless otherwise noted, all Scripture quotations are taken from the New King James Version®. Copyright © 1982 by Thomas Nelson. Used by permission. All rights reserved.

Scripture quotations marked KJV are from the King James Version of the Bible.

Scripture quotations marked NLT are from the Holy Bible, New Living Translation, copyright © 1996, 2004, 2007. Used by permission of Tyndale House Publishers, Inc., Wheaton, IL 60189. All rights reserved.

Septuagint quotations are taken from Lancelot Charles Lee Brenton, *The Septuagint Version of the Old Testament: English Translation* (London: Samuel Bagster and Sons, 1870).

Visit the author's website at jonathancahn.com and booksbyjonathancahn.com.

Cataloging-in-Publication Data is on file with the Library of Congress.
International Standard Book Number: 978-1-63641-152-1
E-book ISBN: 978-1-63641-143-9
Signed edition ISBN: 978-1-63641-171-2

22 23 24 — 9 8 7 6 5 4 3 2 1
Printed in the United States of America

Contents

Part I:

THE

MYSTERY

Chapter 1

The Mystery

Is it possible that behind what is happening to America and the world lies a mystery hidden in the ancient inscriptions of the Middle East?

Is it possible that the ancient entities known as the "gods" are more than fiction and possess an independent reality?

Is it possible that they have returned to our world?

Could these entities lie behind what we see on our television screens and computer monitors, what we find in our shopping centers, what our children are being taught in their classrooms, what our leaders announce and implement? Could they lie behind the current events, news, and movements of our times, and behind what is even now influencing our lives without our realizing it?

Is it possible that one of these ancient entities once paid a visit to New York City and started a cultural revolution that is still transforming our world?

Who are the Possessor, the Enchantress, the Destroyer, and the Transformer? And what do they have to do with what is now taking place in our culture?

Could there be a mystery that lies behind and explains the sign of the rainbow and the reason it is now saturating our culture? And could that mystery go back to the temples of ancient Mesopotamia?

Could the mystery of the gods have actually determined the outcomes and timing of Supreme Court rulings down to their exact days?

Is it possible that the dynamics of ancient mythology have actually played out in our public squares and on our city streets in real time?

Could these gods, or beings, actually be the unseen movers and catalysts of modern culture?

Could they even now, at this moment, be at work transforming the modern world beyond recognition?

What is it all leading to?

We will now embark on a journey beginning with the ancient entities known as the *shedim*. We will remove the veil to uncover the first and most important revelation underlying the mystery of the gods. We will see the ancient transformation concerning the gods that changed world history. We will open up a two-thousand-year-old warning involving a house of spirits and what it foretells concerning the modern world.

We will then see how the gods of the ancient mystery have come into our world. We will uncover the *dark trinity*—and how it has changed our culture.

We will reveal how the gods are working and moving in all that is taking place around us, how they are initiating social upheavals and cultural revolutions, indwelling our politics, transforming our world—and even our lives.

Finally, we will open up the meaning and significance of it all, what it portends, what it will lead to, and what we need to know and do in light of it.

◆◆◆

A warning: The mystery revealed in this book will touch the sacred cows of our culture and age. It will broach that which is deemed unbroachable, speak that which is judged as unspeakable, question the unquestionable, and reveal that which has not yet been revealed.

It will address the most radical and controversial issues of our time, the front lines of cultural upheaval, the catalytic forces that are now transforming society, civilization, history, and life as these have been known.

As it progresses, the mystery will become more intense and more explosive. Thus the latter part of the revelation will be even more so than the first.

At the same time, it will touch these sacred cows and issues in a way in which they are not normally touched, illuminated by the light of a mystery that goes back ages, to ancient times.

What one does with the revelations is in one's own court.

The purpose of this book is to reveal them.

Chapter 2

The Return of the Gods

THE GODS HAVE returned.

They had been away for ages. The ancients had exiled them. They wandered the barren and desolate places, the deserts and wildernesses, the alleyways and ruins, the graves and sepulchres. They haunted the underground, the dark realms of the forbidden, the taboo, and the dead. They inhabited the shadows of the outer darkness.

In their days of glory, they had reigned over tribes and nations, kingdoms and empires. They had subjugated cultures and mastered civilizations, infusing them with their spirits, saturating them with their images, possessing them.

They sat enthroned in marble temples and shrines of wood and stone, by hallowed trees and rivers, in sacred groves, and in mountaintop sanctuaries. Their statues and carved images looked down at their worshippers who approached their altars with offerings and tributes, sacrifices and blood, even human victims.

Kings bowed down before them, priests sang their praises and performed their rituals, armies set off to war and laid cities to waste in their names, and children, the rich and the poor, the free and the slave alike exalted them, worshipped them, entreated their favor, invoked their powers, danced to the drumbeat of their festivals, dreamed of them, loved them, served them, dreaded them, became entranced and seized by them.

But the days of their dominion came to an end. They were expelled from the high places, banished from the palaces of kings, driven out of the public squares, cast out of their temples, and removed from the lives of their subjects.

Their groves were neglected, their shrines abandoned, their altars left in disrepair, and their sanctuaries in ruins. No longer were they worshipped or feared. No longer were their hymns sung, their festivals partaken in, or their holy days observed. No longer were they believed in.

The gods were sent into exile. In time they became memories, echoes, and phantoms. And then they were forgotten.

In the days of their absence, kingdoms had risen and fallen, nations had disappeared, an empire had collapsed, and a new civilization had been born.

The world they had left had disappeared. In its place had risen another that was altogether foreign to them. In their absence, man had charted the earth, vanquished nature, dissected the fabric of life, and codified the universe. The forests were no longer enchanted, the shrines were no longer sacred, and nature was no longer magical. The scientist now wore the mantle of the prophet, and the garments of the priests had been replaced by lab coats. The world had been disenchanted.

It was then, having demystified the earth and awash in his newfound powers, that man decided he had no need of any god. And it was then and by that that the ancient door was set ajar. The long-locked portal of the gods was reopened. Thus was their conjuring, their invocation, and their return.

And so it began. They came back from the desolate places and from the dark and forbidden realms. They came up from the underground and from the dwelling places of the dead. They stepped out from the shadows.

They came slowly at first, as the door had, at first, only been slightly opened. Had their entrance been too rapid, it would have been repelled and the door would have closed. But by entering with measured steps, they were able to keep the door ajar and then open it still wider. And as the shock that followed each of their steps dissipated, the resistance to their return would be overcome.

The world they now entered was unlike the one they had left. In the former world, cities glowed with the light of oil lamps and walls were adorned with carved images. But in the world they entered, cities were illuminated with electrical currents and images of light moved across billboards and movie screens, television sets and computer monitors.

The gods could not rule over the modern world as they had over the ancient, not in the same way. But they would rule over it. They would not return to the high places and groves or to their ancient shrines and temples. They would inhabit the new seats of power by which the modern world was led and make of them their thrones. They would come upon the movers and influencers of modern culture and make of them their instruments.

To gain dominion over the modern world, they could not appear as they had in ancient times. Though there was still a remnant of those who worshipped them and who called them by name, they were of the fringe. To the modern mind the gods did not exist, and few would serve them if they believed they did. So the gods came back in disguise. They altered their appearances. They took on new identities and gave themselves new names. They came as spirits of enlightenment, freedom, and power; they came as secular gods, new gods, alternate gods, gods that granted godhood, gods that denied that they were gods, and gods that declared that there were no gods—they came as gods of the modern world.

And so the gods returned. And having returned, they began working their dark magic, prodding and impelling, tempting and seducing, drawing away, uprooting what was planted and planting what was not, overturning, transforming, moving the ancient markers, breaking down the ancient hedges, and forcing open the ancient gates. And as the seeds of their planting came to fruition, and their spirits infused more and more of the modern world, they grew still more powerful.

And so the gods now dwell among us. They inhabit our institutions, walk the halls of our governments, cast votes in our legislatures, guide our corporations, gaze out from our skyscrapers, perform on our stages, and teach in our universities. They saturate our media, direct our news cycles, inspire our entertainments, and give voices to our songs. They perform on our stages, in our theaters and stadiums; they light up our television sets and computer screens. They incite new movements and ideologies and convert others to their ends. They instruct our children and initiate them into their ways. They incite the multitudes. They drive otherwise rational people into irrationality and some into frenzies, just as they had done in ancient times. They demand our worship, our veneration, our submission, and our sacrifices.

The gods are everywhere. They have permeated our culture. They have mastered our civilization.

The gods are here.

◆◆◆

To begin the mystery of the gods, we must go back to ancient times and to the entities known as *the shedim*.

Part II:

THE

SPIRITS

Chapter 3

The *Shedim*

T HE GODS WERE everywhere.

Planet of the Gods

They haunted the ancient world. The fact that in the past two thousand years they have not been everywhere is an exception to the rule. For most of recorded history the gods were in every land and enthroned on the pinnacle of every major culture and civilization, from the god Enlil of Sumer, to Ra of Egypt, Amarok of the Arctic, Kukulkan of Central America, Wotan of northern Europe, Dionysus of Greece, Obatala of Africa, Tiamat of Babylon, Bixia of China, Oro of Polynesia, Ahura Mazda of Persia, Perun of Russia, Shamash of Assyria, Dagda of Ireland, Juno of Rome, Shiva of India, and a countless multitude of others.

Wherever there were people, there were gods. They reigned over nations, over cities, over cultures, over nature, over the underworld, and over the heavenlies. Their presence permeated the lives of their subjects. The people were bound to them.

That the gods could appear in every land, transcending the many differences, distinctions, and barriers of culture, to become a near universal part of human life is a strange and peculiar phenomenon. To modern sensibilities, the phenomenon of the gods is the product of man's imagination, his projections, his fears, desires, and fantasies. That is certainly part of the story.

But what if there was more to it? What if there was another dynamic in the mix, another realm?

The Devastators

In the Book of Deuteronomy, Moses speaks of a people departing from God and turning elsewhere:

> They sacrificed to *shedim*, not to God, to gods they did not
> know, to new gods, new gods that had come.[1]

In turning away from God, they worship other gods. Those other gods are identified as the shedim. In all the Hebrew Scriptures the word appears only once more, in the Book of Psalms:

> They served their idols, which became a snare to them. They even sacrificed their sons and their daughters to *shedim*.[2]

The word *shedim* again stands for the gods and idols of the nations that the people of Israel turned to when they turned away from God. What does it mean?

Shedim comes from the Hebrew root word *shud*, which means to act violently, to lay waste, to devastate, that which brings destruction. In ancient Babylonian writings the word *shedim* or *shedu* speaks of spirits, protective or malevolent. The latter case would match the root word from which the word *shedim* derives. A malevolent spirit would lay waste and devastate and bring destruction.

The *Daimonia*

When the ancient Jewish scholars rendered the Hebrew Bible into Greek, in a translation known as the Septuagint, they had to find the right word in Greek to stand for *shedim*. The word they used could refer to a spirit, a principality, an occult entity—a god. The word was *daimonion*. It is from this that we get the word *demon*, a malevolent or evil spirit. In the Jewish world the shedim are demonic spirits. So the Septuagint translates Deuteronomy 32:17 this way:

> They sacrificed to *daimoniois*, not to God, but to gods they did not know, to new gods, new gods that had come to them.[3]

And Psalm 106:36–37 is rendered:

> They served their idols, which became a trap for them. They even sacrificed their sons and daughters to *daimoniois*.[4]

Writing to the believers in the city of Corinth, the apostle Paul spoke of the sacrifices offered up on the altars of the Gentile or pagan world:

> ...the things which the Gentiles sacrifice they sacrifice to
> *daimonia* and not to God, and I do not want you to have
> fellowship with *daimonia*.[5]

So Paul writes that when the Gentiles offered their sacrifices to their gods, they were actually offering them to the *daimonia*, the same word used in the Septuagint to stand for the Hebrew *shedim*, the dark or malevolent spirits.

The ancient Greeks viewed the daimonia much the same way that the Babylonians viewed demons—as spirits that could be good or evil, while in the Bible the word is used only to signify spirits of evil.

The words of the apostle Paul in 1 Corinthians are strikingly similar to the words of Moses in Deuteronomy 32 and of the psalmist in Psalm 106. All three Scriptures speak of the spirits, the shedim, the daimonia, as being worshipped and offered sacrifices. In Deuteronomy and Psalms those sacrificing to the shedim are Israelites who have turned away from God. In 1 Corinthians those sacrificing to the daimonia are of the pagan world.

The Entities

All three reveal a connection that is far-reaching and profound. When the Israelites offered up their children as sacrifices, they were doing so on the altars of specific gods. Likewise, the idols to which the Gentile world offered up sacrifices represented specific deities, gods of the pagan world.

In other words, the gods of ancient Canaan and Phoenicia to which the Israelites sacrificed were not simply the figments of pagan imagination but actual spiritual entities. Likewise, the gods that the Gentiles worshipped and sacrificed to in the first-century Roman Empire, gods with such names as Jupiter, Apollo, Vesta, and Bacchus were not simply the imagined or invented characters of pagan mythology—but were connected to spiritual entities, the daimonia, demonic spirits. From the Old Testament Hebrew to the New Testament Greek, the revelation is clear and consistent—behind the gods of the pagan world were the shedim, the daimonia, the spirits.

Worship is connected to spirituality. Spirituality is connected to the Spirit or to spirits. And spirits, as revealed in the Bible, can be either of light or of darkness. Spirits of light are called angels. Spirits of darkness are called demons. And while angelic entities are, by nature, joined to the worship of God, demonic entities are, by nature, at war with the worship of God. They would thus lead one away from the worship of God, even if through the means and form of other gods.

The Ancient Key

Could that which the Scriptures reveal about the shedim and the daimonia provide the key to the phenomenon and mystery of the gods? Could it be the reason behind their universality, why they have transcended the vast spectrum of human culture and have manifested in every land on earth? Could it be the key behind the many similarities and convergences between the cult of the gods and the world of the occult, the overlapping of the ancient pagan rites to the gods and witchcraft?

This is not, of course, to suggest that mythology is real. Mythology is mythology. But is it possible that the mythological worlds of pagan worship contain connections to the spiritual realm, shadows of the shedim and the daimonia? Could the one be affected by the other and the other by the one?

Could the mythology of the gods contain revelation concerning the realm of the spirits? And could the realm of the spirits employ the mythologies of the gods? In other words, is it possible that the mythologies of the gods have, in varied ways and degrees, followed the spirits, the shedim and the daimonia? And is it possible, as well, that the shedim and daimonia, the spirits, have, in some way and to varied degrees, followed the gods and utilized their mythologies for other purposes?

———————◆◆◆———————

Note: From this point forward, when the gods or a specific god is spoken of as possessing agency, consciousness, and will, it is referring to the spirits and principalities that lie and operate behind them.

———————◆◆◆———————

If the gods are spirits and the spirits are gods, then what happens when people or nations are given to them?

Is it possible for entire peoples, nations, or civilizations to become possessed?

Chapter 4

A Civilization Possessed

I F THE GODS of the ancient world were joined to the spirits, then what happened to those peoples and nations under their dominion?

The word *daimonizomai* is used in the New Testament to speak of the effect of a spiritual principality on an individual. It can be translated as "demonized" or "possessed." So if behind the gods of the ancient world were spirits, we would expect the signs of *daimonizomai,* or demonization, to manifest in those cultures that worshipped and served the gods—the signs of possession. And that is exactly what we find.

Seized of the Gods

The phenomenon of possession can be found in most pagan cultures of the world. Where there are gods, there is more likely to be possession. One can find the phenomenon of possession in virtually every region and people group of the world—from the Mesopotamians to the Greeks to the Romans to the Zambians to the Taiwanese to the Eskimos to the peoples of Africa, Asia, South and North America, and Europe. It is another example of a strange phenomenon manifesting in virtually every land and people group on earth. Beyond that, the signs and manifestations of possession as recorded in virtually every culture and land are remarkably consistent.

If behind the gods were principalities, then we would expect that those who especially worshipped and communed with them would be especially vulnerable to possession. And that too is exactly what we find. In fact, in the pagan world the phenomenon of possession was often linked to the gods. The ancient Sumerians experienced the possession of the goddess Inanna. The ancient Greeks experienced the possession of the god Dionysus. The closer one was to the deity, the more in danger one was to possession. The priests and priestesses of the gods and goddesses were especially vulnerable.

What are the signs of possession? The Bible gives several accounts that reveal them. The symptoms of possession include convulsions, shakings, and violent frenzies. These very same signs appear in pagan accounts of the individuals being possessed by the gods. In fact, shakings, convulsions, and violent frenzies were often the most dramatic and striking features of pagan worship.

The Oracle of Delphi

The most famous seer of the pagan world was the high priestess of the Temple of Apollo at Delphi, the Oracle of Delphi. She was known as the Pythia after the mythic giant python that was said to have guarded the sacred site at Delphi. The python gave revelation and prophecy from the gods.

According to Greek mythology, the god Apollo slew the python and established his own temple and his own prophetic oracle on the site. Thus the god took the name of the serpent and became the Pythian Apollo and, as such, would take possession of the oracle and speak through her. For the Greco-Roman world, the Oracle of Delphi was the epitome of divine revelation. Kings and emperors came to Delphi to inquire of her and to receive revelation from the gods.

Signs of the Serpent

In the pagan world the serpent was often seen as a source of divine wisdom. But in the Bible the serpent is a symbol of darkness, of the satanic or demonic realm. Before uttering her prophecies, the Pythia would fall into a frenzied delirium, violently shaking, moaning, shrieking, foaming at the mouth, and speaking unintelligible words. All these are classic signs of spirit possession. And indeed even the oracle claimed to be possessed by a spirit, the spirit of the god. And so the highest realm of revelation in the ancient pagan world was occupied by a woman possessed by a spirit. Again we see the mystery of the shedim and the daimonia. The gods and the spirits moved as one.

Mass Phenomenon

This opens up an even larger truth. If the oracles, the high priests, and the priestesses were possessed of the spirits, and they were each the highest vessels of their nation's spirituality—then what about their nation?

The dominion of the gods and spirits was never confined to the temples and shrines. It permeated entire cultures and civilizations. The deity was not worshipped only in their temples and shrines but in their homes, workplaces, marketplaces, fields, mountains, and valleys. The majority of their worshippers were not priests or officiants but farmers, shepherds, potters, traders, everyday men, women, and children.

So if the culture or kingdom worshipped the gods and the gods were spirits, then the culture and kingdom were joined to the spirits, subject to them, and under their dominion. The signs of possession were not confined to the priesthood or temple. The shakings, the convulsions, and the violent frenzies could manifest anywhere, at any time, and with anyone.

A Civilization Possessed

Beyond the signs of individual possession were other signs and symptoms of a much larger phenomenon. In pagan culture it was not uncommon for people to offer up other people as sacrifices to the gods. In some pagan cultures people even murdered their own children in sacrifice to the gods. They did so as acts of worship. Such things were not the spontaneous acts of a possessed individual but the ways, traditions, rituals, and collective acts of a possessed culture.

The larger truth is that possession may involve more than an individual. It may involve an entire culture, nation, kingdom, or civilization. It is this phenomenon, that of *collective*, *mass*, or *civilizational possession*, that is critical to understand if one is to understand the radical metamorphosis that took place in ancient times, that altered world history, and the equally radical transformation taking place at this very moment.

In the first century, in an unlikely place, a peripheral land of the Roman Empire known as Judea, an unlikely revolution was begun. It would change the history of the gods and of the world itself.

We now journey to that unlikely place and that unlikely phenomenon that brought about the *twilight of the gods*.

Chapter 5

Twilight of the Gods

TWO THOUSAND YEARS ago, in the midst of the Greco-Roman world, in the heartland of Galilee, in the hilltop village of Nazareth, there appeared a Jewish man named Yeshua, who would become known to much of the world as *Jesus*. He came as the long-prophesied Redeemer, the Messiah of Israel, and the Light of the world. He would, in time, become the central figure of human history.

The Galilean

The earliest accounts of His ministry record His performing miracles in the sight of the Judean multitudes. The lame walked, the blind received sight, and the lepers were healed. Another miracle of healing that He was recorded to have performed was described by the Greek word *ekballo*. *Ekballo* means *to expel, to eject, to cast out, to send away.*

The Bible records several encounters between Jesus and those possessed, or "*demonized*" by *unclean spirits*. In each case, He cast out the demonic spirit. In each case, the person was set free, healed, and restored to his or her right mind. Before the end of His ministry on earth, He imparted the same power of *ekballo*, the casting out of spirits, to His disciples.

Emanation

In the fourth decade of the first century, the message of forgiveness, salvation, and eternal life in the death and resurrection of the Messiah, Yeshua, or Jesus, the message that would become known as the *gospel*, went forth from the city of Jerusalem. It spread first throughout the land of Judea. Then it went into the nations, to the Gentiles. The gospel and the Word of God had crossed into the pagan world. That crossing would change the course of world history.

The message of God now entered the lands of many gods and idols. The ways of God now touched the ways of the pagan world. The Word of God now touched the realm of mythology. The Spirit of God now moved through the world of spirits. And the disciples of God now moved through the dominion of the shedim, the daimonia.

Clash of the Gods

If behind the gods were principalities, then when the two worlds met, we would expect an intense conflict. And that is exactly what took place. It was a clash of spirits. The Book of Acts records several of those first clashes. In the city of Philippi a woman possessed with the "spirit of divination"[1] stalked the apostle Paul and his coworker, Silas, for days. Luke, the writer of the account, uses the Greek word *puthon*, or *python*, to describe the possessing spirit. It is the same word used to identify the Oracle of Delphi and the spirit that possessed her—and the god behind the spirit that possessed her.

After several days of being followed, or stalked, the apostle Paul cast the spirit out of the woman. It was that casting out of the spirit that led to a violent backlash. The crowds went into an uproar; the two disciples were arrested, beaten, and imprisoned. Their imprisonment only came to an end when an earthquake shook the prison to its foundations.

In the city of Ephesus, where the disciples proclaimed the Word, performed miracles of healing, and cast out the spirits, the conflict between the gospel and the gods led to a dangerous confrontation. The idol makers of Ephesus stirred up the multitude into a fury against the Word and faith that was being proclaimed. The violent rage was centered on the city's patron goddess, whom they believed was threatened by the new message and faith. The crowd chanted the name of the goddess over and over again as it sought to exact vengeance against the disciples.

Fury of the Gods

The rage of the pagan world against the gospel would grow so fierce that, in time, believers would be imprisoned, crucified, burned, and sent into the arenas to be killed as entertainment before cheering spectators. The fury of the gods and the ferocity of the spirits were now deadly.

In the early years of the fourth century, the Roman emperor Diocletian launched what would become known as the *Great Persecution*. The number of Christians arrested became so great that common criminals had to be released from Roman prisons in order to make room. Beyond imprisonment, Diocletian's persecution would lead to the torture and execution of countless believers in Jesus.

The Great Persecution, with its deadly fury, was rooted in the gods. It was launched on the day called *Terminalia*, the festival of the Roman god Terminus, lord of boundaries and endings. The persecution was intended to bring about the end of faith in Jesus and the termination of His followers. Christians would be commanded to offer sacrifices to the pagan gods. If they refused, they would be imprisoned or killed.

The Oracle's War

But there is a story behind the story. The Great Persecution had its origin in the city of Didyma in the hilltop Temple of Apollo by the Aegean Sea. It was there that the emperor Diocletian sent a delegation to have an audience with the temple's oracle. It was believed that the gods were angry at the new faith. It was believed that the gospel was interfering with the ability of the gods to transmit prophecies to their priests and priestesses. The delegation came with a question for the oracle. The emperor wanted to know whether he should launch a persecution against them.

The oracle's response gave Diocletian the answer he needed. He was to make war against the believers and the new faith. So the greatest persecution of Christians in the Roman Empire was launched by a woman possessed by a spirit, one of the shedim, the daimonia, the spirit of a pagan god.

The Great Exorcism

In the end it was not the gods that prevailed, or the might of the Roman Empire, or the words of the oracle. Against all odds, the overwhelmingly powerless followers of the crucified Redeemer overcame the fires of persecution. And the message of the gospel, of God's love and forgiveness, overcame the reign of the gods. The polytheism and pantheism of the Greco-Roman world gave way to the belief in one God. And the mythological consciousness of ancient paganism yielded to the Word of God and to a salvation that had manifested in time and space. Myth yielded to history.

The spell of the gods was broken. The skies were no longer filled with their thrones, and the earth was no longer their haunting ground. Their names no longer inspired fear and awe. Their festivals attracted fewer and fewer worshippers. Their shrines were abandoned. Their temples fell into ruin. It was the twilight of the gods.

But if behind the gods were the spirits, then when the spell of the gods was broken, we would expect the signs of possession to dissipate. And so they did. The frenzied spirit possessions of the pagan priests, priestesses, oracles, and worshippers became an increasingly rare phenomenon. The carnal and licentious acts of pagan worship and rituals were banned from the public sphere. And human sacrifice became a distant memory.

The Breaking of the Spell

The breaking of the spell and its repercussions went far beyond the realm of pagan worship. The degradation of human life that was typical of paganism yielded before the new belief that life was sacred. The individual was also sacred and so possessed immutable rights. Women were, likewise, sacred and were to be treated as equal heirs of the kingdom. And the poor and the weak were no less created in the image of God than were the rich and powerful. They were to be treated accordingly, as equals. Every life was now of inestimable value and equally precious in the sight of God.

Every realm of society was affected. Sexuality was now to be treated as a sacred gift from God, to be honored and kept in the equally sacred vessel of marriage. As for little children, they were no longer to be abused or mistreated. To take their lives because they were unwanted was now a crime. As for emperors and rulers, governments and kingdoms, they could no longer claim the authority of godhood. They too were subject to God's laws and standards, as was everyone. So the twilight of the gods would transform the Roman Empire and Western civilization.

The Greek word *ekballo*, used in the New Testament to describe Jesus' casting spirits out of individuals, now took on a colossal dimension. The casting out now applied to an entire empire. The gods had been cast out of their temples, their cities and lands, from Western civilization itself. And if behind the gods were the spirits, then the casting out of the gods represented the greatest mass exorcism in world history.

My Hall Has Fallen

What happened to the Oracle of Delphi, the pinnacle of pagan revelation and its most exalted case of spirit possession? In the year 362 the pagan Roman emperor known as Julian the Apostate attempted to restore the oracle's temple to its former glory. He sent a representative to consult her. She sent back a word that would become known as her last pronouncement. It is recorded that she said this:

> Tell the emperor that my hall has fallen to the ground. Phoebus [*the god Apollo*] no longer has his house, nor his mantic bay nor his prophetic spring: the water has dried up.[2]

The gods had been exiled. The possessing spirits had been cast out. No longer could they take possession as they had in earlier days. Nor could they direct empires with their prophetic utterances. Their oracles had grown silent.

Exiles and Exorcisms

It was an end and a new beginning. The driving out of gods and spirits that took place in the Roman Empire would now take place beyond its borders. It would happen in every place in which the gospel was received. Each time it happened, the signs of possession, individual and civilizational, would begin to disappear.

No longer would the Germanic tribes gather in the forests to hang their victims on sacred trees as sacrifices to their god Odin. No longer would the Slavs offer up their prisoners and slaves as sacrifices to their god, Perun. And no longer would the Aztecs tear out the beating hearts of their victims in honor of their sun god, Huitzilopochtli. What had happened in the Roman Empire would be repeated throughout the earth. Civilizations were exorcised. The gods lost their hold, and the spirits departed.

The phenomenon of a civilization set free from the gods and cleansed of the spirits was something new to world history. It had never before happened. The phenomenon was unique to Western civilization. It would radically alter the course of that civilization and then that of the world itself.

The worship of gods may come to an end—but principalities and spirits do not. They go on.

What then became of the gods and spirits?

And if they did go on, could they not one day return?

And if they did return, what would happen?

To bring the mystery into modern times, we must uncover one more ancient puzzle piece.

The House of Spirits

COULD THE LAST clue be found in an ancient parable?

The Parable

The final puzzle piece lies in an ancient passage recorded in the New Testament, the words of Yeshua, Jesus, given to His disciples—a parable within which is a revelation of profound, massive, and prophetic ramifications for the modern world and our own day. He said this:

> When an unclean spirit goes out of a man, he goes through dry places, seeking rest, and finds none. Then he says, "I will return to my house from which I came."[1]

What does it mean? And how does it relate to the matter of the gods? And what significance could it contain concerning modern times?

The House of Spirits

The passage speaks of a man possessed by an unclean spirit. The man is delivered of that spirit. The spirit then wanders through dry places, presumably the desert, but finds no place to rest. It then decides to return to its "house," the formerly possessed man.

But when it returns, it finds that its former dwelling place, the man, is empty, swept clean, and set in order. The cleansed state of the vessel leads the spirit to go and bring back seven other spirits more evil than itself. So the man is now possessed by seven other spirits in addition to the original one. He is thus now in a worse condition at the end than he was at the beginning.

At first glance it would seem that the parable is talking about a possessed and delivered man who then becomes repossessed. It certainly could be applied to a possessed individual. But the parable is actually not about the man at all. It is only an illustration, an example, an analogy used to reveal a spiritual principle and give a prophetic warning.

Spirits of Rome

The key comes in the last words of the parable. After stating that the "last state of that man is worse than the first," Jesus adds, "So shall it also be with this wicked generation."[2] Thus the parable is not about individual possession but collective, or mass, possession, the possession of a generation, a culture, a civilization.

The parable's immediate application appears to be the generation that lived in first-century Judea. But the principles revealed in the parable extend far beyond the age and borders of that nation. They apply to Western civilization as a whole and span the entire age into the modern world. How so?

Two thousand years ago the Roman Empire and Western civilization comprised a house of spirits, a civilization possessed of gods and spirits. But into that house came the Word of God, the Spirit of God, the gospel. Western civilization was thus set free from the spirits and became, as in the parable, a house set in order, a civilization cleansed.

So then what happened to the principalities? The parable answers that. The spirits still exist but now dwell outside the house. So in the case of Western civilization the spirits that once possessed it still existed but now dwelled outside the borders of that civilization. They roamed the dry places, the desolate lands; they dwelled in the shadows. They dwelled in exile.

Return of the Spirits

The spirit in the parable finds no rest. So it seeks to return to its "house" to *repossess* it.

When Jesus was about to cast the spirits out of the possessed man known as the *demoniac*, it is recorded that the spirits pleaded with Him to be cast into a nearby herd of pigs. The spirits are parasitic. They need a host to possess.

Thus the spirits cast out of Western civilization, if they find no rest, if they find no comparable civilization to possess, will seek to return to what they believe is their house. And thus we would expect that the same spirits that once possessed Western civilization would seek to do so again.

But the question must be asked: How could the spirit return to the house from which it has been dispossessed?

The Empty House and the Seven Others

It could only do so if the house has become unoccupied, empty, and the door has been left open. The parable continues:

> And when he comes, he finds it empty, swept, and put in order.[3]

The house is clean and set in order because of its initial deliverance, or exorcism. And yet the implication is that no one is now living there. The house was left empty. Thus it is open to being reoccupied.

> Then he goes and takes with him seven other spirits more wicked than himself, and they enter and dwell there; and the last state of that man is worse than the first.[4]

Since the house is clean, swept, and in order, the spirit brings in seven other spirits to join in the repossession. The implication is that if the house had not been cleansed and set in order, the spirit would not have brought back the other spirits to occupy it.

The Darker State

And therein lies the warning. The house that is cleansed and put in order but remains empty will be repossessed. And if it should be repossessed, it will end up in a worse state than if it had never been cleansed. What happens if we apply this to an entire civilization?

It would translate to this: Should a culture, a society, a nation, or a civilization be cleansed, exorcised of the gods and spirits—but then remain or become empty—it will be repossessed by the gods and spirits that once possessed it, and more. And it will end up in a far worse state than if it had never been cleansed or exorcised at all. It will, according to the parable, end up many times more possessed and evil than before.

The Door to Repossession

But in the case of Western civilization, how would it happen? How would the spirits reenter the house from which they were cast out? How would the gods return?

In the scriptural accounts of exorcism, the spirits are cast out by the Word and power of God and in the name and authority of Jesus. When the Roman Empire and Western civilization were delivered from the spirits and gods, it happened the same way, by the word and power of God and by the name and authority of Jesus.

Therefore, how could the spirits and gods return to Western civilization? Only one way—if that civilization should ever turn away from God, from

His Word, from the gospel, from Christianity, from Jesus. If it should do so, then that which drove out the spirits will no longer be present to protect it against their return. And the civilization that had been delivered of the spirits will become repossessed by them. The gods will return.

Pre-Christian Versus Post-Christian

And what would happen then? According to the parable, the repossessed house will end up far worse than at the beginning. Taken into the realm of world history, it means this: A post-Christian civilization will end up in a far darker state than a pre-Christian civilization. If Western civilization turns away from God, what will come of it will be much darker and far more dangerous than what it was in its days of paganism.

It is no accident that the modern world and not the ancient has been responsible for unleashing the greatest evils upon the world. And it is no accident that when nations and civilizations that had once known God turned away, when they turned against the Christian faith they had once received, what then came upon them would often be described in terms of the demonic.

A pre-Christian civilization may produce a Caligula or a Nero. But a post-Christian civilization will produce a Stalin or a Hitler.

A pre-Christian society may give birth to barbarity. But a post-Christian society will give birth to even darker offspring, Fascism, Communism, and Nazism.

A pre-Christian nation may erect an altar of human sacrifice. But a post-Christian nation will build Auschwitz.

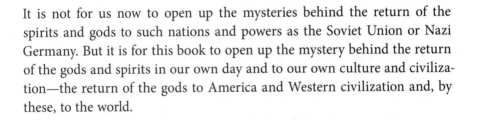

For a nation or civilization that had once known God, that was once delivered of the gods and spirits, to then turn away from God is a most dangerous thing. The gods will return to it.

It is not for us now to open up the mysteries behind the return of the spirits and gods to such nations and powers as the Soviet Union or Nazi Germany. But it is for this book to open up the mystery behind the return of the gods and spirits in our own day and to our own culture and civilization—the return of the gods to America and Western civilization and, by these, to the world.

It is a mystery that touches all of us, just as the working of the gods and spirits is now touching, altering, and transforming the world around us.

————◆◆◆————

If the gods were to return to the modern world and to America, how would they do so?

Is there an ancient template that reveals the answer?

And what is the *dark trinity*?

Part III

THE DARK

TRINITY

Chapter 7

A Word Before the Revealing

WHAT WE'RE ABOUT to see will touch on subjects, issues, and events that are now impacting the modern world. But it will do so in a new light. There are individuals and groups on every side of every issue. This is not about any individual or group—but about the gods, the spirits, and the principalities. The mystery cannot be directed. It exists apart from anyone's opinion, desire, or will. The chips must fall where the mystery will have them fall.

There is no *us* or *them* in what is about to be opened. There is only *us*. The mystery of the gods and the dangers revealed in that mystery apply equally to all and with no distinction.

———————◆◆◆———————

On the walls of the ancient city stood the watchman. If the watchman saw a coming danger, an enemy army, the approach of destruction, it was his charge to sound the alarm and warn the people. If he kept silent, they would perish and he would be guilty of their blood.

The mystery of the gods concerns nations, civilizations, the world and everyone in it. It speaks of life and death, good and evil, danger and the warning of danger, calamity and redemption. To be aware of such things and not reveal them would be to act as a watchman who sees the approach of danger and keeps silent. It would be a moral breach to not reveal it.

At the same time, the revealing of the mystery, as with the sound of a watchman's alarm, will, by nature, cause a disturbance. No true watchman sounds the trumpet to cause a disturbance. He does so knowing that only by sounding it will those who will awaken, awaken and those who will be saved, be saved.

The greatest commandment is love. With regard to what is about to be revealed, there is no room for any other response but love and compassion—for we are all in the same boat. We must stand for what is right and against what is not, we must shine the light into the darkness, and we must do it all manifesting the truth in love.

In the Book of Ephesians the apostle Paul makes clear a critical distinction:

> We do not [war] against flesh and blood, but against
> principalities, against powers, against the rulers of the
> darkness of this age, against spiritual hosts of wickedness
> in the heavenly places.[1]

The book will be the uncovering of those principalities, powers, rulers, and hosts. As they affect all without distinction and as the issues involved are of life and death, the directive of love is all the more critical.

And in this case, love warrants the speaking of truth. Danger warrants the giving of warning. And with regard to the gods, the mystery warrants its revelation.

With that said, we now move to its revealing as we open up the mystery of the *dark trinity*.

Chapter 8

The Dark Trinity

I F THE GODS were to return, if they were to reenter Western civilization, how would they do it? And what gods would they be?

They would not come as they had in ancient times. A modern world requires a different approach. And a world that had been touched by the gospel and had known the Word of God was far different from the pre-Christian and pagan world that had not. So the gods would alter their appearances and hide their identities.

It would begin in the shadows, on the fringes of American society and Western culture. It was there that the gods gained their first footholds. And from there they began their steady and progressive penetration of mainstream culture. But their ultimate object was not infiltration but domination.

The Opening of the Door

The gods could only return if there had been a falling away from the Christian faith and a biblical worldview. No single event or date can be pinpointed as the beginning of that falling away. It was a process. But there were milestones, turning points, and moments of critical mass. In the mid- to late twentieth century America's departure from God became increasingly discernable. The nations of western Europe were in the midst of a similar departure. The falling away would continue through the end of the twentieth century and into the twenty-first, unabated, deepening, widening, increasing in magnitude and momentum.

This time period, the late twentieth and early twenty-first century, represented the most widespread and massive falling away from the Christian faith and morality in the entire two-thousand-year history of the Christian age. The falling away would go hand in hand with the return of the ancient spirits.

America was the leading nation of the era and focal point of the post–World War II order. What would happen to American culture would touch the world. If the spirits could enter and gain possession of the American house, they could possess the age.

The Spiritual DNA

But if the gods were returning, then which gods?

America is not made up of any one ethnicity or people group but many, almost all. In many ways America is a composite and summation of Western civilization. So then what gods could relate not to one nation or ethnicity within Western civilization but to all of them or to Western civilization as a whole? The answer goes back to ancient Israel.

The faith of Western civilization comes from ancient Israel. The Bible consists of the writings of Israel, the psalms of Israel, the chronicles and history of Israel, the prophecies of Israel, and the gospel of Israel. The spiritual DNA of Western civilization comes from and, in many ways, *is* the spiritual DNA of ancient Israel.

Seduced by Other Gods

In the case of America, the connection is even stronger. As Israel was consecrated to God from its inception, so was America. America was established after the pattern of ancient Israel. In its founding days the Puritan leader John Winthrop gave the new civilization a charge based on Moses' charge to the Israelites. If America followed the ways of God, he said, it would become the most blessed, prosperous, and powerful of civilizations. But he also gave a prophetic warning:

> But if our hearts shall turn away, so that we will not obey, but shall be seduced, and worship and serve other Gods, our pleasure and profits, and serve them…we shall surely perish.[1]

So America at its inception was given the same warning that Israel was given at its inception. It was warned against turning away from God and to the gods. It was warned against the seduction of the gods, just as the gods had seduced Israel.

The Gods of Apostasy

And in this is the key that answers the question. The gods, or spirits, that have returned to America and Western civilization are the same gods and spirits that seduced ancient Israel in the days of its apostasy.

In other words, if the nation founded after the pattern of ancient Israel, America, should apostacize from God, then it would become subject to the same gods and principalities that ancient Israel became subject to in its apostasy from God.

The same principle applies on a larger scale to Western civilization. If a civilization indwelled by Israel's faith and word should apostacize from that faith, it would become subject to the same gods and spirits of Israel's apostasy.

The Dark Trinity

So then what were the gods of Israel's apostasy? There were several. But three of them were of special prominence. The three gods embodied the apostasy itself.

One of the three remains something of a mystery. Another of the three was both one and many. And the other changed identities and appearances depending on the time, place, people, and culture. Together they constituted Israel's *dark trinity*.

As for America, though there are many spirits and principalities, it is this same dark trinity that is most prominent in its fall from God, just as it was in Israel's fall from God. As they transformed ancient Israel, they are now transforming America and Western civilization, and through this, the world.

The Re-paganization

Pagan spirits inhabit pagan vessels. Pagan gods indwell pagan cultures. What would happen then if the ancient pagan gods returned to a civilization based on a Judeo-Christian foundation, worldview, and moral framework? What would happen is that their return would trigger a metamorphosis. The Christian, or biblically based, culture would begin transforming—into a pagan one. Christian values would be replaced by pagan values, Christian ethics by pagan ethics, and a Christian worldview by a pagan worldview. We would witness the paganization of American civilization, and the re-paganization of Western civilization.

We now uncover the mask behind the first of the three gods, the dark trinity—*the Possessor*.

Part IV:

THE

POSSESSOR

Chapter 9

The Possessor

H E WAS THE king of gods, leader of spirits. And he would become the chief enemy of the God of Israel.

Lord of the Clouds

He was the god of fertility. His worshippers prayed to him to make fertile the soil and cause their crops to grow. They called him *Lord of Rain*, master of the waters that caused the earth to bear fruit. He was the god who rode on the clouds, the lord of storms. He was the one who hurled down bolts of lightning on the earth. If he prospered, the land prospered. If he languished, so did the people.

He was a warrior. He would enter into battle with his fellow gods over and over again. In the end, though, he would reign supreme over his pantheon.

It was the role he played with regard to the nation of Israel for which he is most known and notorious. And it was that role that concerns us with regard to the mystery.

The Master

He was called *Baal*, chief god of the Canaanite pantheon. His name can be translated as "lord," "owner," and "master." The Bible speaks of both *Baal* and the *Baalim* or the *Baals*. He was one and, at the same time, many. Nations, regions, and cities each had their own *Baals*. There was Baal Hadad, Baal Hermon, Baal Tamar, Baal Peor, and Baal Zephon, among many others. Even families had their own personal *Baals*, clay figurine idols of the omnipresent deity.

The Alternate God

It was not long after the Israelites settled the Promised Land that they began turning away from God.

> Then the children of Israel did evil in the sight of the LORD, and served the *Baals*; and they forsook the LORD God of their fathers, who had brought them out of the land of

Egypt; and they followed other gods from *among* the gods of the people who were all around them, and they bowed down to them.[1]

Baal promised the Israelites fertility, fruitfulness, increase, gain, and prosperity. Thus as they began cultivating the land, the temptation to invoke his powers proved more and more compelling. Many Israelites turned away from God to follow him.

He was so prominent that when the Bible mentions his name along with those of other foreign gods, he is almost always mentioned first. To the people of Israel, he was the head of the *"other gods"* and was, himself, the quintessential *other god*.

In the ninth century BC the worship of Baal had made such inroads into Israel's culture and state that those who refused to join it were persecuted, hunted down, and killed. It was over the worship of Baal that the prophet Elijah rose up against the apostate king Ahab and his co-regent, Jezebel.

Years later, after the nation's destruction, the Scriptures would cite Israel's worship of Baal as central among the reasons for the calamity. No other deity was so connected to Israel's falling away from God and its subsequent destruction as was Baal.

Baal and Zeus

In later days Baal, in his incarnation as *Baalshamen*, or *Baal Shamim*, was identified with the god Zeus, head of the Greek pantheon. An ancient Nabatean text says this:

> ...they regarded as god the lord of heaven, calling him Beelsamen, which is in the Phoenician language "lord of heaven," and in Greek "Zeus."[2]

Syriac writers referred to *Baalshamin* as *Zeus Olympios*. Both gods appeared as idols standing in the same position, with arms lifted up and ready to hurl a thunderbolt to the earth. Zeus was presented as *Zeus Belus*, and Jupiter as *Jupiter Belus*, which could be translated respectively as "Zeus Baal" and "Jupiter Baal."

And so when the gods were cast out of the Greco-Roman world, Baal Shamin, or Jupiter Belus, was one of the exiled deities.

The Anti-God

To the nation of Israel, Baal was the embodiment of paganism and of all pagan gods. He was the epitome of all that was not God and all that warred against Him. Baal was the *other god*, the *substitute god*, the *instead of God*. He was Israel's *anti-God*. He was the god that Israel turned to when it turned away from God. He was the god who separated Israel from its God, who drew it away, who made it forget the God of its foundation.

◆◆◆

So if Baal was the god of the turning away, the god of the falling, the apostasy god, what would happen if he returned to the modern world?

What would happen if he came back to possess a nation, a civilization?

What would happen if Baal came to America?

Chapter 10

The Possessor Returns

HOW DOES A god of the ancient Middle East make his way into a twentieth-century Western nation? How would Baal come to America?

Baal Comes to America

What would be the sign of his coming? Baal was the god of apostasy. His mission was to take a nation that had known and been consecrated to God and turn it away from God, estrange and alienate it from the God of its foundation. As Baal was the chief of the "other" gods in Israel's apostasy, he would be the first in America's apostasy and the one to lead the way for the others.

The turning of a nation away from God and to the gods often begins with the smallest of steps and an almost imperceptible shifting. But any opening is enough for Baal to get in and then push the door further ajar. In the case of ancient Israel, it would seem a little thing to add prayers to Baal alongside the worship of God to increase one's prosperity. But it would not stay little.

The Once and Other America

In the mid-twentieth century the majority of Western nations were still viewed as Christian or Judeo-Christian. And America was decidedly and proudly so. It stood in clear opposition to Marxist ideology and the atheism of Soviet Russia and Communist China.

America was a nation in which even liberal newspapers would publish summations of sermons preached throughout the city the previous Sunday. Its leading magazines could advocate for Christian morality and Christian revival. Its entertainment was expected to uphold biblical and Christian values and to never attack them. And it was not a strange thing for its television stations to sign off at night with a sermonette or prayer.

It was a nation in which the majority of those on the political Left and Right saw themselves as sincere followers of Jesus or God and in which politicians would freely cite God and Christian values in their public discourse.

America in the mid-twentieth century was a nation in which children were not only allowed to pray in public schools but actually led in prayer by their teachers, and where teachers read the Word of God in their class-rooms. And it was an America that declared itself *"one nation, under God."*[1]

It was into that nation that the spirit of Baal came.

The Ancient Amnesia

How does that spirit come into a nation that has known of God? The Book of Judges reveals how it began in the case of ancient Israel:

> They forgot the LORD their God, and served the Baals and Asherahs.[2]

In the Book of Jeremiah, written in the last days of that apostasy, the voice of God laments over the nation's spiritual condition:

> Their fathers have forgotten my name for Baal.[3]

The mission of Baal is to cause a nation that has known God to stop knowing Him and then to forget Him, and then to forget that it ever knew Him. The spirit of Baal caused Israel to forget the God of its foundation and become estranged from Him. By the end of the process it could no longer remember or imagine what it was like to have known Him.

The American Amnesia

And so when Baal returned to the modern world, his mission would be the same—to cause America and the West to forget its God. How would he do that?

After the destruction of Israel, or Samaria, in 722 BC, the Bible gave a requiem for the fallen kingdom:

> And they rejected His statutes and His covenant that He had made with their fathers, and His testimonies which He had testified against them; they followed idols, became idolaters....So they left all the commandments of the LORD their God, made for themselves a molded image and two calves, made a wooden image and worshiped all the host of heaven, and served Baal.[4]

The people were drawn away from the Word of God, the laws of God, and the ways of God. In the case of America, Baal would use the same strategy. He would first seek to separate the nation from the Word and ways of God.

The Banishing of God

Though the seeds of America's turning from God can be found in earlier days, it would become most noticeable and would achieve critical mass in the 1960s. It was at the beginning of that decade that America removed prayer from its public schools. The act was soon followed by the banning of God's Word from the instruction of the nation's children. The Bible had always been part of the American public school system, from its beginnings at Massachusetts Bay. Thus the change was a monumental one—and with regard to the spirit of Baal, a strategic one.

Children of Baal

When Baal was unable to possess one generation of Israelites, he would focus on the next—the nation's children. Since children represent the future, if he could take hold of America's children, he could take hold of America. So by removing prayer and the Word from the education of America's children, he was weakening the transmission of faith to the next generation. He could then separate the entire nation from prayer, from the Word, and from faith. By causing God's ways to become alien to the nation's children, he could cause the alienation of America from God.

The Baalization of America

Baal's American agenda was not limited to its school system. It would permeate every sphere of American culture. Its major newspapers would no longer publish summations of the past Sundays' sermons, its leading magazines would no longer endorse Christian values, its entertainment would no longer uphold biblical morality, its politicians would speak less openly of Christian values, and its television stations would no longer promote prayer or present the ways of God in a positive light but would now war against them. Praying to God or mentioning the name of Jesus in the public square would be increasingly viewed with hostility.

The nation was becoming increasingly alienated from the ways of God.

A War of Tablets

The law that God gave Israel was a safeguard against the gods and the ways of paganism. The very first of the Ten Commandments was, "You shall have no other gods before Me."[5] So for Baal to gain possession of Israel, he had to separate the people from the Law of God and, as it was summed up, the Ten Commandments. The writer of 2 Kings confirms what happened:

> So they left all the commandments of the LORD their God.[6]

The Ten Commandments and the Law were also at the foundation of Western civilization. In the case of America, they were specifically cited as the cornerstone on which the new society was to be built. So for Baal to gain possession of America, he would do just as he did to ancient Israel. He would cause them to put away the Ten Commandments and depart from the ways of God.

So in 1980 the Supreme Court ruled that it was no longer legal to display the Ten Commandments in public schools. They were what the American school system had once taught and lifted up as the nation's moral foundation. Now it was illegal to even make them visible in public.

But the conflict would not end in the halls of America's public schools. The nation would strike down the Ten Commandments more than once. The Ten Commandments would come under governmental judgment and be banished from the public square.

The Schizophrenic Nation

Baal had turned Israel in upon itself. He caused the nation to war against its own foundation. His fingerprints could now be seen on an America at war with its own foundation.

The fingerprints of the ancient god could be seen in the Supreme Court, which had ruled against the display of the Ten Commandments and yet displayed the Ten Commandments on its very walls.

They could be seen in the presidential inauguration as the president-elect placed his hand on the Bible to swear the presidential oath and then, upon becoming president, enacted laws and policies that warred against the ways of the Bible upon which he swore.

They could be seen in the nation's school system, which instructed the nation's children against the very ways for which that school system had come into existence.

And they could be seen on the nation's currency, which was increasingly used to eradicate God's presence and ways from American public life and upon which were written the words "In God we trust."

Baal had done to America as he had done to Israel; he turned it in against itself. It had become as had ancient Israel, a civilization in spiritual schizophrenia.

The End of "Christian America"

Since the Word and law of God served as safeguards against the gods and paganism, their removal opened the door for the gods to come in unhindered. America had removed from public view the commandments against worshipping other gods—now it could do so. It had removed the commandments forbidding sexual immorality—now it could embrace it. It could now indulge in all that the commandments had warned against.

Once the Word of God was removed, there was nothing left to hold back the nation's fall, no absolute standard. The guardrails were down. There was now nothing to stop what would soon follow. The nation was left wide open to the subjection and dominion of the gods.

The America where prayer and God's Word were imparted to its children, where Scripture was revered in its media and culture, and where the ways and precepts of God informed its laws and national policies and were proclaimed in the public square—was no more. Observers would now write of "the end of Christian America."[7]

Baal had succeeded. America was going to be altered beyond recognition.

———————◆◆◆———————

According to the parable, an empty house is a dangerous thing. America had emptied itself of God.

It would not remain empty.

Others would come in.

Chapter 11

An Exchange of Gods

COULD THE ANCIENT parable of spirits hold the key to what is now taking place in America and Western civilization?

As the gospel entered into Western civilization, the gods departed, the spirits left the house. It was the advent of Christianity, the Word and presence of God, the ascendancy of monotheism over paganism that caused their departure. But if these things should be weakened or removed, then the departed spirits and ancient gods would return.

The Door Left Open

And so it began. The hedge protecting American civilization was progressively weakened. The moral and ethical framework derived from the Scriptures was overturned. So the two primary safeguards against the gods, and that which, in ancient times, had cast them out—monotheism and the Word—were now being nullified. The door that had closed to the gods would be reopened.

In his mythologies, Baal entered into battle against other gods, and not only against the gods of Canaanite mythology but against the God of Israel and His people, against all who kept His ways. His battle was waged in the realm of morality, spirituality, politics, and culture. So in late twentieth-century America the return of Baal would bring about a cultural, civilizational, and spiritual collision. It would, at times, be described as a "culture war," but it was much deeper than culture. The conflict was ultimately spiritual, that of Baal against God—the rematch of an ancient battle.

In and Out

He came in via a spirit of openness and a call to embrace new ideas and ways. But his entrance would ultimately result in the progressive closing of the nation's openness to God. Every step the nation took to accept the "new morality" would be matched by an equal and opposite step toward the rejection of God and His ways. What was once seen as the source of virtue and freedom and joy was now viewed as a hindrance, a restraint, an oppression.

As Baal had been cast out of the Jewish world and then, by the gospel, out of Western civilization, he would now seek to cast God out of America. What had been done to the gods in ancient times would now be done to God. America and the West would begin casting Him out.

It would happen subtly at first but in time would deepen and widen and continue into the twenty-first century. God would be driven out of the halls of government, out of the public square, out of movie theaters, out of television sets, out of the arts, out of ethics, out of hearts, out of minds, and out of lives.

Empty Houses and Returning Spirits

But the ancient parable held an ominous warning for America and the West. The house, having been emptied, would not remain empty. Having cast out God, the gods would come in to replace Him. Having expelled the Spirit of God, other spirits would take possession. Baal would make America his home. He would be the spirit that, in the parable, then ushers the other spirits into the house. And so America's turning from God in the early 1960s would usher in other spirits and gods and a future that no one at the time could have imagined.

The law of the ancient parable would manifest in virtually every realm of American culture. When the nation removed prayer and the Bible from its schools, to some observers it seemed a small thing. But the removal left the house spiritually empty. And according to the parable, it would not remain empty. Other spirits would come to replace what was cast out. What would, in time, come into American classrooms would have been unimaginable to those alive at the time of the emptying. The nation's children would now be trained *against* the ways of God. The American school system had become a house of spirits.

Baal Goes to Hollywood (and Everywhere Else)

So too American movie screens, having been emptied of God, would now be filled with that which was once forbidden and that which warred against the ways of God. It would happen to American television, American universities, American popular music, American youth and children's culture, American corporations, American houses of government, even some American houses of worship. Everything was darkening. The nation's institutions, having been emptied of God, were turning into houses of spirits.

And it was not only the nation's institutions. America itself was now becoming a house of spirits.

————◆◆◆————

Could Baal actually manifest in America as he did in ancient Israel—
in physical form?

Chapter 12

The Molten Beast

BAAL WAS THE god of prosperity. As the Lord of rains and fertility, he represented increase, gain, and profit. The belief that he could bring fruitfulness to one's fields and vineyards was among the strongest of his appeals and weapons in his battle against the God of Israel.

American Idols

The lure of Baal had always been a present danger in American culture. For any nation so blessed with material prosperity as was America, there would always be the risk that its prosperity would become an idol and that it would turn to the god of increase and gain. But with America's departure from God in the late twentieth century, the spirit of Baal became ascendant.

Unlike the ancient apostasy, the spirit would not be centered on the fruit and yields of the earth but on their modern equivalents—financial seeding and yield, monetary profit, increase, and gain. It had the trappings of a new religion, a cult of success, and a doctrine of materialism and greed. In the Scriptures, God is called *"the Almighty."* In a revealing choice of words, America dubbed its own currency *"the almighty dollar."*

The spirit of Baal could not be contained in the halls of business. It was everywhere. Americans pursued money, served money, were driven by money, and worshipped money as much as the ancients had worshipped their idols. American life became increasingly monetized. The spirit of Baal even went to church. As in ancient times, when Baal worship was added to the worship of God, so now the doctrines of Baal, the pursuit of material prosperity and personal gain and success above all things, invaded the sanctuary. And so what could have been a protection and antidote against the invasion was compromised.

The Bull God

Baal was typically portrayed as a bearded and helmeted figure, holding a spear of lightning in his upraised hand. Some of his images show the horns of a bull coming up from his head or helmet. Baal's preeminent symbol was the bull. The bull embodied his power and his connection to fertility.

So his idols came in the form of the helmeted man but also in the form of a bull of metal or clay.

It was America's financial realm and, in particular, its stock market, and, more in particular, Wall Street, that epitomized the unadulterated pursuit of money. It was there that the spirit of Baal as it related to a nation's yield and prosperity most clearly manifested. The prosperity of the stock market had long been tied to the prosperity of America as a whole. It was therefore striking that the symbol that had come to embody the prosperity of the stock market and America—was the bull.

Of course the bull did not come to Wall Street because anyone was seeking a connection with Baal. Nevertheless, it did come. And the fact that the symbol of American prosperity was the same ancient symbol of national prosperity and that it was so without any conscious intent is even more striking. If the American stock market appeared heading toward increase, gain, and prosperity, it was the market of the bull, the bull market. So Baal's ancient symbol became not only an American symbol but one that embodied the same realm and dynamic as it had in ancient times.

The *Egel* and the Apostasy

But the appearance of the bull in ancient Israel was a symbol, as well, of something else—a nation's apostasy from God. More specifically, the bull was the symbol of a nation that had once known God, that had once been consecrated to His ways, but now had forgotten Him. It was the sign of a nation that had rejected Him to follow other gods. So it was in ancient Israel, and so it would be again in America.

The younger version of the bull was also critical in Israel's history. The Hebrew word *egel* refers specifically to a young bull, a male calf, also known as a *bull calf*. In Israel's apostasy from God at Mount Sinai, the people created a golden *egel*, a bull calf. So the calf, or young bull, became the symbol of national apostasy.

The Sign of a Nation's Departure

Centuries later Jeroboam, leader of the rebellion that split the kingdom of Israel in two, erected two golden calves, one at each end of his kingdom. He then called his people to worship them as their gods. The bull, or bull calf, again became the sign of a nation's fall from God.

The apostasy at Sinai and of Jeroboam involved an image of molten metal. So too the worship of Baal involved the making of molten bulls for the purpose of worship. So Israel, in its fall from God, worshipped bulls and calves of molten metal. After the destruction of Jeroboam's kingdom, the writer of 2 Kings would write:

> So they left all the commandments of the LORD their God, made for themselves a [*molten*] *image*...and served *Baal*.[1]

Thus the sign of a nation that has left His commandments, His Word and ways, is the appearance of the molten image, and specifically the molten image of a bull, or a young bull, the bull calf. If America was now the nation that was departing from God and if the spirit of Baal had now come to indwell it, is it possible that the sign of Baal would follow?

If the image of a molten bull was to appear in America and be linked to the same spirit to which it was joined in ancient times, the spirit of materialism and gain, it would be a sign of a nation that had once known God but had turned away and was now worshipping another god—Baal.

Materialization

The sign appeared.

The site of its materialization was the financial district of New York City, just outside the New York Stock Exchange on Wall Street. It appeared in December of 1989. It was massive, eleven feet tall and sixteen feet long. It weighed seventy-one hundred pounds. It was a molten image in the form of a giant beast—a bull—the sign of Baal.

It would later be moved to a location where it could stand as a permanent landmark of New York City. But it would remain in the city's financial district, not far from the stock exchange, and the most massive and concrete symbol ever to represent Wall Street. Thus the sign of Baal, the god of increase and gain, would be linked to the New York Stock Exchange, America's house of increase and gain.

The image was described as a "symbol of aggressive financial optimism and prosperity."[2] The words themselves were a modern recasting of the power of the ancient god. Though meant to encourage the nation, the sign was menacing. The bull's nostrils were flaring as if ready to attack. One observer described the molten creature as "an angry, dangerous beast." Another described it as embodying an "aggressive or even belligerent force."[3]

The Other Image

On the day it appeared on Wall Street, the bull was not alone. There was another image overlooking it. It was the statue of the nation's first president, George Washington. The bull appeared on the ground on which America came into existence as a constituted nation. It was there that Washington was sworn in as the nation's first president.

After being sworn in, Washington delivered a prophetic warning. He said, in effect, if America ever turned away from God and His eternal laws, its blessings would be removed.[4] It was an echo of Winthrop's earlier warning against ever turning to other gods, "our pleasure and profits."[5] And now, standing across from the statue that commemorated the day and place in which Washington gave that prophetic warning against turning away from God, was the sign that the nation had done exactly that—it had turned away from God.

The American Baal

So the sign of Baal that had once appeared in the high places and sacred pagan grounds of the Middle East now appeared in America. As in ancient times, it appeared in molten metal. In fact, the ancient bulls of Baal were often of molten bronze. So the bull that appeared in New York City was also of molten bronze.

It was the American incarnation of Baal. It was, as well, the American version of the golden calf, the ancient biblical sign of a nation that had once known God and had fallen away, and that another god had mastered it.

◆◆◆

In ancient Israel the molten bull constituted a tangible image and sign of the possessing god. But his impact and effect upon the nation was much deeper. What about the return of Baal to the modern world? What was his deeper impact on America and the West? It is that to which we now go as we uncover the paganization of America and modern civilization.

Chapter 13

The Deep Magic

I F A NATION changes its God, the nation itself will be changed. So as America turned from God to the spirit of Baal, a transformation took place. The ancient god began working his deep magic and set in motion the paganization of American and Western civilization. It would happen on a multitude of levels, some brazen or overt, others not as obvious but deeper, under the surface and, in the end, even more profound and far-reaching. These were the deeper consequences of America's paganization.

Gods, *Isms*, and Auras

When Israel turned from God, the land became filled with idols. It was not an accident. It is an unchangeable dynamic. The nation that turns from God will always turn to other gods. Even if it never utters their names or erects their idols, even if it turns to atheism or a form of secularism, it will always be led to the worship and serving of other gods. The dynamic can be seen in Communism, Nazism, Fascism, and any other *ism* that seeks to drive out God. Other things will take on the aura and authority of godhood and seek to reign in His place.

The reason is simple: when God is removed, the need to worship Him remains, even in the modern world. And if that need is diverted from Him, it will go elsewhere. If a nation or civilization turns away from Deity, then all things become subject to deification. Or in other words, if nothing is God, then anything and everything is God. So it was not only that Israel turned to Baal; it also turned to the Baalim, or the many Baals.

Most Americans would never admit to turning to such things or creating idols. Nor would they utter the names of the gods. Nevertheless, as did Israel in its fall, America now turned to worship its own American gods and fashioned its own American idol.

Deification

As America turned from God, it began deifying the objects of its culture. The worship, the passion, and the energy that had once infused its devotion to God were now redirected to that which was not God. And that which was not God now became sanctified, empowered, and enchanted.

Substitutes for God had always existed, but now, with the expelling of God, they began taking on the garb of deity. In the absence of God there was nothing that could not be deified.

One's god is that which is one's ultimate reality. Therefore, it cannot be questioned. So there now arose new movements, causes, ideologies, and systems of thought that could not be challenged or questioned—no matter how irrational they were—since they were now gods. Rather, one had to bow down before them, whether the gods were of *political correctness* or *wokeness* or a multitude of others. As faith was removed from God, it was given to other things. New ideologies came in to fill the void and rule as gods as their movements took on the characteristics of religions.

The worship of Baal was one of carnality and vulgarity. So as America turned from God to Baal, its culture underwent a process of vulgarization. Its national discourse turned increasingly crude; its entertainment, increasingly carnal; and its overall culture, increasingly profane.

The Fabrication of Truth

The spirit of Baal works toward the altering of perception. Where there is one God, there is an ultimate and objective reality, a unifying reference point and standard by which all can be discerned, measured, and judged. Where there is God, there is truth. But where there is more than one God, or many gods and Baals, the door is open for many truths, conflicting truths, and thus no truth.

When one makes an idol, one is fabricating one's own god, and thus one's own ultimate reality, and one's own truth. But when one creates truth, truth becomes a fabrication and ceases to be truth. And when one creates or holds to one's *own* truth, truth again ceases to be. Two plus two cannot equal four for one person and five for another. So one of the signs of Baal's subversion of a culture is that the culture will turn away from objectivity to subjectivity.

And so as America and Western civilization turned away from God, they began undergoing a process of subjectification. As they moved away from the truth, they moved away from the concept of truth itself, that there was any truth to begin with. The transformation affected language. Truth was now what was true for the individual. If a man believed he was not himself but was someone or something other than what he was, a child, a woman, a leopard, or a tree, there was no ultimate or absolute truth or any truth, no objective reality to contradict his own personal "truth." And if one's personal truth contradicted reality, then it was reality that would have to be bent into conformity.

The Overturner

And so without God there was no more truth and, in fact, no more reality. Words were now redefined. What was right was now wrong, and what was wrong was now right. Values were altered. People were altered. And reality was forced to bend its knee before the new idols or else become the clay to be molded into the image of the new gods.

So by the spirit of Baal the eternal truths were overturned. Values and standards that had stood for thousands of years were now discarded with a single vote of a legislature or a president's executive order. And the foundation stones of Judeo-Christian civilization could now be struck down by a single ruling of the nation's judiciary.

Of course, any position that denies truth and the existence of absolutes must ultimately contradict itself. It will, in the end, assert its own absolute truth. But even this was a sign of Baal's spirit. It was the other side. If one can turn the absolute truth into what is subjective, then one can turn the subjective into absolute truth.

The very act of creating an idol or a god is to forge out of nothing a new absolute. And so in the absence of God, American culture forged new truths, created new laws and commandments, and molded new absolutes out of the molten metal of its apostasy. And as it was in ancient Israel when Baal came into power, those who would not bow down before the new gods and idols would be punished, canceled.

The Gods Repackaged

But it was not only polytheism, the belief in multiple gods, that characterized paganism—but pantheism, the belief that all was God. And so the return of Baal would also bring about the return of pantheism. It could be seen in the secular or materialistic belief that there was nothing other than or more than the world or the universe. Thus the physical world was the ultimate reality. The world was God, and God was the world.

And it was no accident that as America began driving God out of its life, it began opening itself up to other spiritualities. Several of these fell under the umbrella of New Age teachings, movements, sects, and practices. But behind the new veneer and modern packaging was ancient paganism.

Some of the streams of New Age movements and teachings had a distinctly polytheistic bent. Some involved the conjuring of spirits. Others involved the invoking of ancient gods and goddesses.

But other streams were distinctly pantheistic. God was all, and all was God. Beyond the return to paganism, the embrace of New Age beliefs often represented a turning to Eastern beliefs and a further departing from the Christian and biblical faith.

But it was the more imperceptible penetration of pantheism into American and Western culture and consciousness that would prove to be more profound and pivotal. Even those who saw themselves as Christian were often unwittingly affected as their thinking and perceptions were subtly altered.

Worshipping Gaia

Baal led Israel into the worship of nature. So it is no accident that it was at this same time, of apostasy and the spirit of Baal, that American and Western civilization began to embrace the worship of nature. Nature was no longer a gift from God to be stewarded. It was now the ultimate reality. The earth would be christened with the name of the ancient goddess Gaia, and the world would be deified.

Man was of nature, nature was God, man was God, and God was everything—pantheism. Distinctions were eradicated, and lines were crossed. One of these lines was that between man and animal. This too went back to Baal.

The Rise of the Animal Men

As we have seen, Baal was depicted in both human and animal forms. It was typical of paganism, in its mythology and imagery, to merge form, to mix humans with animals, one species with another. While the Hebrew Scriptures emphasized uniqueness and distinctions, the pagan world nullified them. So as the spirit of Baal came upon America and the modern world, lines that had never been crossed were now breached, and distinctions that had undergirded society and life were eradicated.

Whereas ancient artisans had merged man and animal in images of stone and clay, modern scientists now merged them, but not through molding clay or chiseling stone, but by molding and splicing the genetic code. The distinction between man and animal was increasingly blurred. The offspring of animals could now be given rights and protections that millions of human babies were never afforded. And man was increasingly viewed as something of a glorified animal. It was one of the unvarying effects of Baal and the gods. They degraded all who worshipped them and debased all who served them.

The Drowning Lifeguard

The bending, blurring, and breaking of distinctions characteristic of the pagan world began seeping into nearly every corner of American culture and life. The distinctions between right and wrong, life and death, the natural and the unnatural, man and woman, good and evil—they were now blurring, bending, and breaking.

It was all born of the same root, the pagan confusion and merging of the Creator and the creation, God and man. If the world was God and man was one with the world, then man was God. As God, he could nullify reality or create another. He could even re-create Himself. He could make the unnatural natural and the natural unnatural. He could alter values, turn right into wrong, evil into good, and good into evil.

But if man had become God and God was the world, then there was nothing else. Then there was nothing beyond the world to give meaning to life or purpose to existence. And if the world was broken and the world was God, then God was also broken. And then there could be no repair. And if man was lost and man was God, then God was lost and there was no hope of redemption. And so the dismal emptiness and hopeless despair of ancient paganism began creeping back into Western civilization and darkening it. For how could there be any hope of redemption or salvation if the one drowning was the lifeguard.

Under the deep magic of Baal, America was morphing into something altogether alien to what it had once been and once stood for. As he had done to ancient Israel, he was now doing to America. The leader of Christian civilization was becoming distinctly pagan. Baal had turned America into its own antithesis.

Could an ancient word lie behind our most advanced technologies, and an ancient mystery lie behind the rise of the computer?

Chapter 14

The Masters

WHEN THE PEOPLE of Israel turned from God, they turned not only to the gods, but to a specific kind of god:

> They sacrificed to the Baals, and burned incense to carved images.[1]

They turned to the Baalim. Who or what exactly were the Baalim? In order to answer that, we must first define what exactly the gods and idols were to the people of the ancient world—and what they are to us now.

The Identity of a God

With regard to the worshipper, a god or idol is that which one ultimately worships, serves, and lives for. It is that which one most focuses and dwells on, and from which one takes the greatest joy. It is that which one most reveres and is led, moved, and driven by. It is one's ultimate reality and the purpose of one's life.

So if one turns from God, there will always be another, a god or an idol.

The Baalim

The Hebrew word *Baalim* literally means the "Baals." The Baalim was Baal in his plural form. He had appeared in a multitude of forms and variations and was embodied by a multitude of idols. So Baal was manifested through the Baals. The word *Baalim* can also be translated as "*the lords*," "*the owners*," and "*the masters*." If one turns away from God, one will end up serving the Baalim, or one of the Baalim, a god or an idol that will end up becoming one's master, one's owner, and one's lord.

Having turned from God, Israel became subject to the Baals, the new lords and masters. The Bible records that the Israelites *served* the Baalim. The Hebrew word translated as "*served*" also means "*to labor under*," "*to be kept in bondage to*," "*to be enslaved by*." Their apostasy began with the promises of prosperity, fulfillment, and liberation. But it would end in bondage.

Lords of America

So too for America. The lure of the Baalim was the promise that turning away from God would bring freedom and fulfillment. But instead, it led to enslavement, to the bondage of the Baalim. And as in ancient times the Baalim appeared in a multitude of forms.

So Americans now served and were mastered by the Baals of money, pleasure, success, acceptance, sexual gratification, addictions, work, comfort, the internet, self-fulfillment, self-obsession, and countless other gods and idols—the Baals of the modern world.

Instead of freedom, Americans saw their culture becoming increasingly driven, restless, conflicted, obsessed, and addicted. And the further the nation moved from God, the more powerful the Baalim became. To America, devoid of God, the pursuit of money and success became an unbridled spirit that possessed millions. With Americans devoid of God, the pursuit of pleasure led to a multitude of addictions and self-destruction.

The Altars of Baal

The Israelites offered up sacrifices to the Baalim. So did the Americans. For the Baalim of money and success, they sacrificed much of their lives. For the Baalim of pleasure, they sacrificed their well-being, their health, their marriages, their families, and their children. The new, modern Baalim were more than ruthless masters—they were deadly.

Of Israel's fall to idols, the prophet Isaiah wrote:

> Their land is also full of idols; they worship the work of
> their own hands.[2]

That was the irony of idolatry. They worshipped as gods the very thing that they themselves had created, *"the work of their own hands."* They had created their own Baals.

The Mars Hill Mystery

When the apostle Paul came to Athens, a city filled with gods, altars, and idols, his spirit was, as recorded in the Book of Acts,

> ...provoked within him when he saw that the city was given
> over to idols.[3]

When he later stood on Mars Hill before the city's leaders, he addressed the worship of idols:

> Therefore, since we are the offspring of God, we ought not to think that the Divine Nature is like gold or silver or stone, something shaped by art and man's devising.[4]

He was using the same argument presented by the prophets. They were worshipping that which they themselves had devised, what their own hands had made.

In speaking of the creation of idols, the apostle used the Greek word *techne*. From that same word, linked to the idols of man, we get the modern word *technology*. In other words, *technology* comes from a word used in Scripture in connection with idols.

The High-Tech Idol

America was largely responsible for ushering in the age of high technology and for creating the modern computer. The computer represented the most sophisticated and advanced work of man's hands, the most advanced form of man's techne. And in the age of apostasy, it has become among the most powerful of man's idols and the most complex of the Baalim.

Under the spirit of Baal, the Israelites worshipped and served the works of their hands. Under the spirit of Baal, America did likewise. The ancient idols were deaf, blind, and mute, unable to move or act. But the high-tech idols of the modern world were more powerful; they could see, hear, and speak, and do almost anything. And each generation became more attached to them, more plugged in, and more addicted to them than the generation before. And each found it harder to break free of their spell.

The Breach of Reality

In the pagan world it was not only the god who was worshipped but the idol, the image of the god. The idol and the god were one. Image became reality; reality became image. So in the paganization of America and modern culture, the line between image and reality was likewise breached. Image became reality, and reality became image. More and more people were living more and more of their lives in a virtual world, a world of fabricated virtual reality.

The virtual became increasingly real, and the real became increasingly virtual, just as truth became increasingly virtual. American and modern culture was now saturated with a flood of images and sounds that signified nothing—a hymn to the idol.

They Will Become Like Them

The Book of Psalms reveals a profound truth concerning the dynamic between the worshipper and the idol:

> Their idols...have mouths, but they do not speak; eyes they have, but they do not see.....*Those who make them are like them.*[5]

In other words, the one who makes, serves, or worships an idol will end up being transformed into its image. So the new technological idols, the digital Baals, would begin altering the nature of man. Computers began taking on human functions, abilities, and similitudes. Artificial intelligence was increasingly rivaling human intelligence and taking over its functions. At the same time, man, increasingly joined to his computer, began taking on the qualities of his digital master. The more one was joined to a computer, the more one began functioning as its appendage. So computers became more human, and those joined to them became less and less so. As the ancient warning of Scripture had foretold, those who made them had now become "*like them.*"

The Machine Man

The line between man and machine was blurring. There was more and more talk and experimentation involving merging man and technology, whether through digital implants or other technological enhancements of human abilities. The line became even more blurred as people began having sexual and romantic relationships with robots.

But even this was part of the ancient mystery of paganism and the gods. In paganism man creates gods and worships the works of his hands; the creator worships his creation. The line between creator and creation is blurred and breached. So if technology is the creation of man, then the pagan blurring and merging of God and man will be manifested in the blurring and merging of man and his technology, creator and creation, man and machine—a hybrid of both.

American and Western civilization had now created the most powerful of idols. And the present generation, more than any other, now served its own creation, its new master, the techne of its own hands. It was the day of the new masters—the age of the technological Baalim.

————◆◆◆————

An object appeared in the streets of New York City. It was shrouded in mystery, covered in a sheet. Most of the city's inhabitants had no idea what it was. The city would unveil it.

The object was linked to an ancient god, and to the dark trinity.

Chapter 15

The Arch

BEYOND THE MOLTEN bull another sign of Baal appeared in America, and again in New York City. And on the day of its appearing, the city would hold a celebration in its honor.

Baal's role in Israel's fall was critical. The nation would be destroyed, but Baal would go on. He was worshipped throughout the Middle East up to the first centuries of the present age. In the first century, in the city of Palmyra, in what is now Syria, a temple was built for his worship. A century later a second temple of Baal was built in the same city, nearby the first.

The Temple of Baal

The first would be known as the *Temple of Baal*, or the *Temple of Bel*, after the god's Babylonian name. The second would be known as the *Temple of Baalshamin*, referring to the god as the *Lord of the Heavens*, or the *Baal of the Sky*. Both temples would remain standing for nearly two thousand years.

Less than a hundred years after the building of the Temple of Baalshamin, a monumental arch was added, the Arch of Palmyra. It was built to connect the Temple of Bel with the city's main colonnaded avenue. The arch was the gateway through which the inhabitants of Palmyra would enter in order to worship their supreme deity. It stood in between the two temples.

In the spring of 2015 the jihadist organization Isis invaded Palmyra. After gaining control of the city, its soldiers began the systematic destruction of the city's ancient buildings and artifacts. After surviving nearly two thousand years of history, the two temples of Baal were destroyed, as was the arch between them.

The Mystery Object

In September of the following year, a mysterious object appeared in New York City, mysterious as it was shrouded in white cloth so no one could actually see it. It was massive, nearly eleven tons of Egyptian marble and rising nearly twenty feet from the ground. It was an arch, a massive re-creation of the arch that led to the Temple of Baal.

It had appeared in London and would later appear in other Western cities, including Washington, DC. But the appearance of the arch that had served as the entranceway to Baal's Temple in New York City was especially significant. For New York City had played a central role in America's apostasy from God and, in many ways, served as the capital of that fall. It had functioned as a conduit for Baal's entrance into American civilization.

City of Baal

And it was New York City in which stood America's modern equivalents to the temples of Baal, its houses and monuments of materialism, increase, and gain. It could even be said that New York City was itself a spiritual Temple of Baal.

Even the location of the arch within the city was significant. It was erected in Lower Manhattan at the entrance to the city's Financial District. Nearby was Wall Street, the New York Stock Exchange, and the other sign of Baal, the molten Bull of Wall Street. As the Arch of Palmyra once stood as the entranceway to the Temple of Baal, the arch in New York City now stood at the entranceway to America's temples of Baal.

And as the ancient arch had connected Baal's temple with the city's main avenue, the re-created arch stood by New York City's most famous and main avenue, Broadway, the modern equivalent to the Great Colonnade at Palmyra. So too did the molten bull; the two symbols of Baal were joined.

The specific site chosen for the arch was also significant. It was erected on the grounds of City Hall, New York City's central seat of government. And the city officials would take part in its unveiling.

The Unveiling

On the morning of September 19, 2016, New Yorkers gathered around the arch for a special event—its unveiling and presentation. By the arch stood a sign placed there by the event's sponsors on which the name of Baal appeared. Among the speakers at the unveiling was the city's deputy mayor, who described the erection of the arch as an "act of defiance."[1]

Providing the ambience for the event was a band playing Middle Eastern music evocative of the sounds that would have accompanied the music played in ancient times in the Temple of Baal. It was to those

Middle Eastern sounds that the massive sheet covering the object was pulled away and the arch revealed to the applause of the gathered spectators.

Baal on Capitol Hill

One can find incidents of Baal worship in the earliest days of Israel's history, as early as its entrance into the Promised Land. The incidents served as a warning of the greater apostasy that would come in later times. So too America's relationship with Baal and even with his temples in Palmyra began long before the Arch of Palmyra appeared on its shores.

In 1753, after an expedition to the Middle East to Palmyra, the British scholar Robert Wood published *The Ruins of Palmyra*. The book would influence English and American architects of the era. It is believed that through that book the elements of the ancient Temple of Baal in Palmyra were incorporated into the US Capitol Building. It is also believed that from one of the drawings in that book, that of an eagle from one of the temples of Palmyra, came the Great Seal of the United States.

As with Israel, so with America, the potential for national apostasy was there from the beginning, the shadow of Baal, embedded in the nation's spiritual DNA. America had been conceived after the pattern of ancient Israel. And so if it turned away from God, in that day, the spirit of Baal would enter in. And now it had.

Baal's Portal

And so the nation that had turned to Baal received the sign of Baal in the form of a massive stone arch. The entranceway to Baal's Temple was placed at the entranceway to American civilization.

And that the arch would appear in other Western capitals was also a sign. The civilization that had once identified itself with the faith of ancient Israel was now being marked with the sign of Baal, the god by which Israel had fallen away from its faith—the sign of a civilization now waging war against the ways of God.

The arch was the gateway to and from the worship of Baal. Its reappearance was the sign of a nation and a civilization that had given him a portal and welcomed him back—a sign that that nation and that civilization had now become a Temple of Baal.

————◆◆◆————

Could an ancient event that took place by a desert mountain contain a prophetic revelation and a critical warning concerning what is now taking place in America and Western civilization?

And could that revelation and warning be embedded in the walls of the American government?

Chapter 16

The Golden Calf Civilization

BEFORE WE MOVE to the second god of the dark trinity, we must return to an ancient mountain for one more revelation.

The Prototype

The first case of national apostasy recorded in Scripture was that of Israel's fall at Mount Sinai. While Moses stood on the mountaintop receiving the Ten Commandments, the people of Israel waited at the mountain's base. Growing impatient at his delayed return, they decided to make a god of molten metal in the image of an *egel*, the bull calf. After creating the idol, they held a celebration in its honor. They feasted and drank with music and festivity, offered up sacrifices on its altar, and as the Scriptures record, "*corrupted themselves.*"[1] Then came judgment.

What happened at Sinai was a prototype and template of national apostasy. The template is now replaying in America and Western civilization. The central elements of that prototype have reappeared—the departure from the Word and ways of God, the rejection of the Ten Commandments, the process of deification, the worshipping and serving of idols, and the replacement of God with a flood of sensuality and licentiousness. And in the case of America, we may add in the actual creation of a molten image of the bull family and the actual striking down of the Ten Commandments.

The Face of Moses

There is another element from the apostasy at Sinai—the face of Moses, gazing down in anguish at his nation's fall. There is on Capitol Hill, in the chamber where the House of Representatives convenes, a face. It is a unique face, the only full-faced representation in that chamber. In fact, all the other faces in profile are turned to it. It is the face of Moses. It gazes down at the speaker's podium. It looks down at the chamber's proceedings, voting, and passing of legislation, and, at the State of the Union address, on the president.

The face of Moses also appears on the walls of the nation's highest court. The most prominent figure on the Supreme Court's eastern side is that of Moses holding the two tablets just as he did on the mountaintop on the day of the Golden Calf. The tablets appear as well on the doors that lead into the Supreme Court Chambers.

So as Moses looked down on Israel's apostasy from Mount Sinai, he now looked down from Capitol Hill and the nation's highest court. He looked down on the House of Representatives when it sought to enact laws that warred against the laws of God. He looked down on the president when he sought to advance an agenda to overturn the ways of God.

Days of the Golden Calf

He looked down from the Supreme Court with the Ten Commandments in hand as the Supreme Court struck down the Ten Commandments in the public square. He looked down on the podium in the House Chamber when the officiant dedicated the new congress to the pagan god Brahma. He looked down on America as it descended into apostasy as he had looked down on Israel as it descended into apostasy on the day of the Golden Calf.

The nation that had been founded after the pattern of ancient Israel had now fallen after the pattern of Israel's fall. It had turned from God and given itself to the gods. Darkness had become light. Light had become darkness. Sin was now holy, and holiness was sin.

Everything was inverted. And Baal, the god of inversion, had done it. He had worked his dark magic.

And the words of the prophets concerning ancient Israel now spoke to America and Western civilization: *they had forgotten His name for Baal.*

That which had been consecrated to God at its inception was now possessed by His enemy. For it could not be forgotten that the name Baal also meant *the Possessor.*

◆◆◆

Baal was the first. He opened the door. But he was not alone.

He had a wife, or mistress.

We now move to the next of the returning spirits, the second god of the dark trinity, and the mystery of the Enchantress.

Part V:

THE

ENCHANTRESS

Chapter 17

The Enchantress

THE SECOND GOD of the dark trinity was a she. She was among the most potent of gods and among the oldest, having first appeared in ancient Sumer.

The Goddess

She was so important among the gods of the ancient Middle East that she was given the title *Queen of Heaven*. She was joined to the celestial lights, to the moon, which some of her mythologies name as her father, and to the sun, which was often named as her brother. But it was another celestial light with which she was most associated, Venus.

She was the goddess of sexuality. It was because of that connection that the planet Venus is associated with love. She was also the goddess of war and destruction. She was fiery, impetuous, impulsive, greedy, emotional, demanding, stormy, fierce, carnal, given to rage, romantic, vindictive, full of unbridled passion, insatiable sexual desire, and boundless pride. If denied the object of her desires or if offended, she would become vengeful and violent and could wreak havoc and destruction.

The Transgressor

She was the breaker of rules, the trespasser of boundaries, and the transgressor of standards and conventions. She would demand that which belonged to others. In one myth, when the gods were unaware, she stole their sacred possessions. In another, she demanded entrance into the land of the dead, the underworld, and pounded on its gates, threatening to break them down if her will was refused. In another, she demanded that the gods give to her the Bull of Heaven to bring revenge on her enemies and threatened that if her demand was denied, she would release the dead into the world of the living.

She was the goddess of prostitution. The prostitutes of ancient Mesopotamia looked to her as their patron and protector. And it was not beyond the goddess to take on the appearance, nature, and function of the prostitute herself.

Seductress

She was a seducer, a temptress, the goddess who captivated, allured, and snatched away. As the patron goddess of the tavern, or alehouse, she was associated with the partaking of alcohol, particularly of beer. She dwelled in the taverns and there mixed sexuality with intoxication.

In Sumerian mythology her foremost lover was named *Dumuzi*. In Assyria and Babylon he was known as *Tammuz*. It was her anger toward him that brought about his death. She then wept inconsolably over her loss. But she was never a faithful wife or lover. Tammuz was one of many. In the famous Mesopotamian poem *The Epic of Gilgamesh*, the goddess even sought to seduce the story's hero, who responded by spurning her advances. She was the goddess of sexual promiscuity.

Enchantress

Her images were everywhere in clay idols and stone reliefs. She often appeared as naked or as a woman revealing herself. She often appeared next to her symbols, the moon or crescent, the sun, and her *star*, which was associated with the planet Venus. And she was often depicted in her function as goddess of war, brandishing weapons and entering into combat. It was undoubtedly because of this role that she was associated with the lion. It would often appear in her depictions as symbols of her ferocity and power.

She was also an enchantress, a sorceress, a goddess of magic and spells. She specialized in love magic, the enchantment that conjured desire or that altered one's affections and behavior. She seized and possessed her worshippers. She moved and spoke through her priestesses, who served as her vessels.

Priests and Prostitutes

Her cult reflected her nature. Her worship was saturated with carnality, sensuality, and open sexuality. Ancient writings speak of her temples as akin to houses of prostitution. It is believed that every year on the tenth day of the Mesopotamian New Year's festival of *Akitu*, the Babylonian kings would perform ritual sex acts in her temple. Whether these acts involved the consummation of sexual union or rather a symbolic form of union is still debated. This would take place through the goddess's high priestess, who would act as her surrogate.

Her ritualized "temple sex" was not confined to kings and high priestesses. According to the writings of the ancient Greek historian Herodotus, the women of Babylonia were compelled by religious custom to sit in the temples of the goddess and perform the function of prostitutes, having relations with a stranger in exchange for money. According to Herodotus, *"Every woman of the land"* was compelled to perform the act at least once in her life.[1]

From such practices come the concepts of *"sacred sex,"* *"temple prostitution,"* *"cult prostitution,"* and the *"sacred prostitute."* All these were especially connected to Ishtar. Such things might be expected of a deity who was so linked to prostitutes or a prostitute herself.

And yet it went still further. Even writers of ancient times, those familiar with the practices of her cult, described them as disgraceful and infamous. Her proclivity to flout conventions and break rules would make her the goddess of those on the fringes of society.

Ishtar

She was among the most ubiquitous and protean of deities. She was able to modify her appearance or trappings to adapt to new peoples, cultures, and lands. In the Bible she is called "Ashtoreth." She is also spoken of in the plural form of her name, "Ashtaroth."

As with Baal, she was everywhere. She manifested in differing forms in different cities, regions, and lands, and her idols could be found throughout the Middle Eastern world. In Canaanite mythology she was connected to Baal and appears often as his wife or consort.

Her influence was so great and so pervasive that one can see facets of her nature, her roles, her functions and attributes in a myriad of goddesses from the Middle East, the Mediterranean, and beyond.

In the Canaanite and West Semitic world she was called *Astarte*. The Sumerians called her *Inanna*. In Assyria, Babylon, and much of the Mesopotamian world she was known as *Ishtar*.

To the Greeks she became *Aphrodite*. At the same time, her young lover Dumuzi, or Tammuz, became the god Adonis. And to the Romans she became the goddess *Venus*. Thus the planet behind the *Star of Ishtar* would be named after the goddess's Roman name.

Ishtar in Exile

We will refer to her as a single goddess and spirit. Though her other names will, at times, appear in this book, the goddess will most often be called by the most famous of her Mesopotamian names: Ishtar.

When the Christian faith entered the Roman and Middle Eastern world, the goddess, along with the other deities and spirits, was cast out. In an age that saw the covenant of marriage as sacred and sexuality as a gift exclusively given and belonging to that covenant, a principality and cult devoted to carnal desire and unbridled sexuality could not be maintained. The goddess went into exile.

But what if she was to come back?

————◆◆————

What if Ishtar was to return to the modern world—and specifically to America?

What would happen?

Could she set in motion a transformation just as massive and critical as that set in motion by Baal—or even more so?

Chapter 18

The Enchantress Returns

How did the second principality enter into America and the West? To find the answer, we must look back at how she gained entrance into ancient Israel.

Mrs. Baal

It was early on, soon after the Israelites settled in the land, that they began turning to other gods. The first record of its turning is found in the Book of Judges. The passage speaks first of the Israelites' embrace of the Baalim, or Baals—then it says this:

> They forsook the LORD and served *Baal and the Ashtoreths.*[1]

From the very beginning, the two gods, Baal and Ashtoreth, or Ishtar, were linked together. The connection reappears later on in the Book of Judges:

> Then the children of Israel again did evil in the sight of the LORD, and served the *Baals and the Ashtoreths.*[2]

It appears as well in the Book of 1 Samuel when the people realize the consequences of their apostasy:

> Then they cried out to the LORD, and said, "We have sinned, because we have forsaken the LORD and served the *Baals and Ashtoreths.*"[3]

The Baal-Ashtoreth Connection

Why are the two joined together?

The fact that they could be portrayed in their mythologies as married or as lovers would account for some of it. But the connection between the two gods is deeper and one that transcends mythology. So too is the order in which their names appear. It is Baal who is first and then Ashtoreth. Israel first turned to Baal and then to Ashtoreth. *Baal leads to Ashtoreth.*

Baal represented the nation's turning away from God and to the physical, the material, the carnal, and the sensual. It was this that opened the door for the entrance of Ashtoreth, or Ishtar, and with it unbridled sexuality, licentiousness, and decadence. The worship of Baal had elements of all these things, but Ashtoreth was their incarnation. The one god ushered in the other, and the one spirit, the next. The god of the apostasy ushered in the goddess of sexual licentiousness and debauchery.

Ishtar Comes to America

What would this mean for America and the West? If America's turning from God began to manifest in the early 1960s and, with it, the entrance of Baal, we would then expect this to be followed by the entrance of Ashtoreth, or Ishtar. And what would then happen in the wake of that entrance?

We would expect a transformation to begin that would alter the realm of sexuality. With the goddess's entrance we would expect biblical standards and ethics surrounding sexuality and marriage to begin to erode. We would expect the moral foundations and values that had undergirded Western civilization for nearly two thousand years to begin overturning.

In short, we would expect there to be a revolution in the realm of sexuality—a sexual revolution.

Ishtar and the Sexual Revolution

And that is exactly what took place. Shortly after America's turning from God began manifesting in the early 1960s, another transformation took place in the realm of sexuality. It would be one of the central defining movements of the 1960s, and it would continue long after the decade was over. It would not stop until it had transformed American and Western culture beyond recognition.

The effect of the goddess's return to America could be summed up in three words—*the sexual revolution.*

There had been another sexual revolution. It took place in ancient times in the Greco-Roman world. It was the revolution by which biblical sexual ethics, ideals, and morality replaced those of the pagan world. It happened at the same time the gods were cast out of Western civilization. The two phenomena were connected.

The casting out of the gods included the casting out of the Roman Venus, the Greek Aphrodite, the Phoenician Astarte, and the Mesopotamian Ishtar, all the varied manifestations of the goddess of sexuality. It was in the goddess's departure that biblical values replaced pagan ones and the first sexual revolution took place.

But if the goddess should return, it would mean that pagan sexual values would now overturn biblical ones. In other words, the sexual revolution that took place in America and Western civilization in the late twentieth century was the reversing of the sexual revolution that took place in ancient times. It was the advent of the gospel that broke the goddess's spell. But now, upon her return, the spell would be cast again—on America, the West, and the world.

The Spell of the Sorceress

The sexual revolution was another dimension of the paganization of America and Western civilization. The values it represented were pagan values, and the sexuality was pagan sexuality. What was branded as the *"new morality"* was in actuality an old morality, an ancient morality, the morality of the gods. The reappearance of that morality was a sign that the departed spirits had returned to the house.

The aim of the goddess was to destroy the morality and faith by which she was expelled. To do that, she would have to take a Christian nation and civilization that, with regard to sexuality and marriage, upheld biblical morality and practices and lead it into embracing pagan morality and practices. To do that, as with the return of Baal, she would have to work incrementally, step by step, and progressively. But it was the spirit of Ishtar. And to Ishtar especially belonged the powers of seduction and spells. So in recasting her ancient spell, she would begin the seduction of America and the modern world.

◆◆◆

What would it mean if America were to come under the spell of an ancient goddess?

Chapter 19

The Great Seduction

WHAT EXACTLY WOULD happen if the spirit of the goddess took possession of a culture? What would happen if it took possession of America?

And Then Came Ishtar

In the American and Western culture of the mid-twentieth century, sexuality was seen as the sacred domain of marriage, and marriage as the sacred and lifelong covenant of love between a husband and wife. These values were largely the same as they had been in ancient times at the advent of Christianity.

Sex outside of marriage, whether premarital or extramarital, was seen as sin. Divorce was frowned upon. If a woman became pregnant before marriage, she and the child's father were expected to marry. The divorce rate was minuscule. So was the percentage of people living together outside of marriage, as was the rate of children born out of wedlock.

Prostitution existed but was illegal and confined to the underworld. Pornography was taboo and, for the most part, kept out of mainstream culture and public view. Even those who broke such standards would, for the most part, keep their behavior private.

American entertainment and popular culture were expected to uphold the same values. Beyond allusion and suggestion, sexual relations were generally not depicted on the movie screen. Hollywood was expected to follow an agreed-upon code of morality as to what could and could not be shown, and it did. Nudity of any kind was forbidden. Any allusion to sex outside of marriage was not to be portrayed in a positive light. And for television screens, the parameters were even tighter.

And then came Ishtar.

The Deification of Sex

We have seen the dynamic of deification—when an individual, nation, or civilization turns away from God, that which is not God will become as God and will assume the aura of godhood. One of those things that are not God is sex. When Israel turned away from God, sex, in the form of the goddess Ashtoreth, or Ishtar, was deified. Sex became a god. Sex thus became an end and a goal to be pursued in and of itself. Therefore, it could now be divorced from marriage or any other context and be followed with no regard for context or any other thing.

When the spirit of Ishtar came to America, the same dynamics began to replay. Sexuality was deified. It became a god to be pursued as an end in and of itself and without regard to marriage, love, or even a relationship. That which was once the exclusive domain of husband and wife now spilled into the public sphere and popular culture.

And so began the progressive severing of sexuality from marriage. As Israel worshipped and served the goddess of sexuality, so now America, indwelled by the same spirit and the same goddess, became increasingly obsessed with sex.

The Destruction of Marriage

Though Ishtar was involved in the ritualized marriage ceremonies of Meso-potamian religion, and though some of her myths involved a form of marriage, there was almost nothing about her that was conducive to marriage. Just the opposite, her nature and acts, her worship and cult, would under-mine it. She was never faithful. She was promiscuous. She pursued and seduced lover after lover. She pursued sexual relations apart from marriage and to the detriment of marriage.

So the effect of Ishtar's return to the modern world was the progressive undermining and weakening of marriage. As sexuality was glorified as an end in and of itself, marriage was eroded. As Ishtar had pursued relation-ship after relationship, so America began doing the same. As the taboo against ending one's marriage began to end, so did marriages. Under the spirit of Ishtar, divorce became an epidemic and America was filled with broken homes.

Passions of the Goddess

Ishtar was led only by her will and desires. She had no regard for the con-sequences of her actions. The idea of denying her desires for the sake of a covenant was to her an anathema. She sought the immediate fulfillment of every impulse. She was the goddess of instant gratification.

So with the return of Ishtar, American and modern culture became consumed with instant gratification. Americans increasingly chose their desires over relationships, over preserving their marriages, or entering into them in the first place. A culture of hyper-individualism, self, and self-gratification proved to be toxic to marriage and relationships.

As it was Ishtar's nature to choose sexual pleasure and romance over commitment, more and more Americans did likewise. They slept with each other, lived with each other, but would not commit to each other. Marriage as a lifelong covenant was increasingly viewed as an unnecessary constraint. What was once fornication now became premarital relations and, in time, the norm. The number of Americans living together without marriage and the number of children born out of wedlock or without fathers would skyrocket.

Ishtar in Hollywood

The realms of entertainment and popular culture were subject to the same spirit. The codes and standards that had been established to serve as moral hedges were now removed. What was once forbidden, abhorrent, or taboo now filled movie screens. And whereas the television industry once avoided showing married couples in bed, now it regularly portrayed unmarried people in bed and having sex with multiple partners. And whereas nudity was once never seen in public, it was now displayed on movie screens and piped into American living rooms.

If Americans from the 1950s had turned on their television sets to see what would appear on the nation's television sets years into the future, they would not have been able to process it. It would have appeared to them as something out of the apocalypse or a dark fever dream. That was how radically effective the work of the goddess had been.

The Taboo

Ishtar's nature was to trespass boundaries, transgress convention, and break taboos. So American culture became possessed by a spirit of transgression, a drive to push the next boundary, to transgress the next convention, to break the next taboo. What was once abhorrent now became a source of pleasure. And it was not only the taking of pleasure in sin but in the breaking of taboos and the overturning of the next standard. It was the pleasure of defilement and desecration.

Not only did Ishtar introduce, promulgate, and champion sexual immorality—she *sanctified* it; she declared it holy. Sexually immoral acts were part of her cult and worship, performed as rites in her temples and shrines. So in the grip of her spirit, the same thing began manifesting in American and Western culture. Sexual immorality was now not only accepted but treated as sacred.

Sanctifying the Forbidden

Now it was the former standards and restraints that were seen as sinful, puritanical, repressive, and evil. And the one who opposed the newly sanctified sins or failed to adequately revere them was now treated as something of a heretic, and the opposition to the new morality as something akin to blasphemy.

What the spirit of Baal had begun, the spirit of Ashtoreth, or Ishtar, had taken to another level. The work of each god was to bring about the inversion of civilization. Ishtar had inverted the realm of sexuality. She had taken what was forbidden, unspoken, and taboo and, step-by-step, introduced it into the mainstream culture. The shock of each step would be followed by familiarity and numbness, then toleration, then acceptance, and then celebration.

At the end of the process, Americans would be championing what they had once forbidden and forbidding what they had once championed. Ishtar's realm was most critical. It was from sexuality that came marriage, family, society, civilization, and life. And so the workings of the goddess would produce the most profound of transformations in American, Western, and world civilization. She would alter them beyond recognition. She would alter life itself.

♦♦♦

Could that which now saturates the world of entertainment, drives major portions of the American economy, and floods the worldwide web go back to a mystery contained in the tablets of ancient Mesopotamia?

Chapter 20

The Sacred Prostitute

SHTAR WAS THE patron goddess of prostitutes. She was their protector, their encourager, their supporter, their guide, and their matron. From the ladies of the night who walked the streets of Sumer to the *"sacred prostitutes"* who inhabited the shrines and temples of Babylonia, they all looked to Ishtar, prayed to her, worshipped her, and were her servants.

Prostitution was a part of her cult. Sexual acts attended her worship and rituals and could be found in her sanctuaries. The temples of Ishtar were famous for their connection to prostitutes and even for the business of prostitution. The connection was intrinsic to the goddess's identity.

The Harlot Goddess

Ishtar was not only the great benefactor of prostitutes but their role model. Her obsession with sexuality, her promiscuity, her countless relationships and lovers—all of these served as examples for the ancient Middle Eastern prostitute.

In the tablets of Sumer, Ishtar, or her earlier incarnation as Inanna, is described as a *"harimtu"* or *"karkid."*[1] The words are commonly translated as *"prostitute."* Some argue that the words can mean prostitute but not necessarily in every context. But the words appear in descriptions of Ishtar where the context clearly refers to prostitution—specifically when it cites the tavern, the place where prostitutes gathered and worked. One ancient hymn says this:

> They cannot compete with you, Inanna [*Ishtar*]. As a prostitute you go down to the tavern and, like a ghost who slips in through the window, you enter there.[2]

And from another:

> You, my lady, dress like one of no repute in a single garment.[3]

As the ancient Mesopotamian prostitute could be identified by her jewelry, so too Ishtar:

The pearls of a prostitute are placed around your neck.[4]

Another ancient tribute to the goddess is even more detailed, as it deals with the pricing of her trade:

When I stand against the wall, it is one shekel.[5]

Another ancient inscription has the goddess saying outright:

I am a prostitute.[6]

The Sexualization of American Culture

The return of Ishtar was the return of the prostitute goddess. It would set in motion a transformation based on the dynamics of her trade as well as her cult of worship.

Prostitution takes sexual relations out of the exclusive context of husband and wife and brings them into the larger culture, into the marketplace, the realm of trade and commerce. Likewise, Ishtar's cult of worship took sexuality out of the private realm of the marriage covenant and into the public realm of festivals, rituals, and temple worship.

So when the spirit of Ishtar returned to Western civilization, it worked toward removing sexuality from the bounds of marriage. Sexuality now moved out of the private realm and into the public realm. What had once been the exclusive possession of husband and wife within the covenant of marriage now became the possession of the larger culture, popular culture, and public life. So American and Western culture became sexualized. Its sexuality had been stolen from the marriage bed. Sexuality was now everywhere and unbridled by the covenant of marriage.

The Harlot's Pay

It was not only that Ishtar's prostitutes would take sexuality out of the marriage bed and into the streets of Sumer and Akkad—they would bring it into the marketplace. They converted it into a commodity to be bought and sold. In prostitution sex was employed as a means of procuring money.

So upon her return not only did the prostitute goddess flood the culture with sexuality, but she increasingly employed it in the marketplace as a commodity. Sex would increasingly be used to procure money, on movie screens, in music videos, in magazines, on the internet, and wherever else it could generate money.

What the spirit of Ishtar had promoted in the cities of Mesopotamia it now promoted in America and world culture. Sex was monetized.

The Pornification of Culture

It was not only that sex was used to sell other commodities, but, as in Ishtar's ancient craft, sex itself was up for sale. Industries that had existed in the shadows now entered the American and Western mainstream and were normalized. Adult magazines, adult clubs, adult movies, adult entertainment increased in numbers and influence. One no longer had to venture into the corners and shadows of American life; the shadows were overtaking America.

The tablets of ancient Mesopotamia contain inscriptions in which the goddess seeks to tempt her lovers into sexual relations. They will not be quoted from here, as they could best be described as pornographic literature. So as the spirit of the goddess increasingly took hold of American and Western culture, pornographic literature and story lines began entering into the mainstream.

As the ancient Mesopotamians read or listened to the pornographic words and stories of Ishtar, Americans now read pornographic literature and watched pornographic movies in theaters, on their television sets, and on their computer monitors.

And as prostitution depersonalized sexuality, so the spirit of the prostitute goddess increasingly depersonalized sexuality.

Mother of Eros

The newly mainstreamed sex industries would employ and be known by the word *erotic*—erotic literature, erotic dancers, erotic massages, erotic movies, erotica. The word *erotic* comes from the word *eros*. *Eros* was the ancient god of the Greeks. The name means desire. *Eros* was the god of sexual desire and love. Eros was born of Aphrodite. Aphrodite was the Greek incarnation of Ishtar. So behind the name given to describe the deluge that was sweeping over American and world culture was the pagan god Eros. And behind Eros was Ishtar. Behind it all was Ishtar. Having returned to the modern world, the goddess had again given birth to Eros.

The Images

The worship of Ishtar was not limited to pornographic literature or story lines. It found its most popular expression in imagery. The image of Ishtar as a naked woman could be found all over the ancient Middle East, in terra-cotta reliefs, royal seals, and clay idols. Images of naked women were typical of pagan culture and especially prominent in the worship of Ishtar.

Thus we might expect that the entrance of Ishtar into America and modern culture would bring a revival of naked imagery. And that is exactly what took place. Naked images, particularly those of women, would again permeate Western civilization. In the modern case it would be known as pornography. In ancient times Ishtar caused images of naked women to spread throughout the Middle Eastern world, in clay, stone, and paint.

Now, upon her return, she began causing the same images to permeate the modern world in photographs, films, video clips, and digital imagery. The images and practices that once characterized the culture of the goddess now characterized American culture.

The Porn Goddess

Among the oldest writings in world history are the "sacred" hymns to Ishtar/Inanna in which she is described as a prostitute. The Greek word for writing is *graphos*. The Greek word for Ishtar's profession, prostitution, is *porne*. It is from this root, "*writings about a prostitute*," that we get the word *pornography*.

Thus by the literal definition of the word, pornography was birthed in the "sacred writings" of the goddess.

And so as the spirit of the prostitute goddess moved upon America, America became filled with pornography, or, as it was called in short, porn, meaning, in effect, "*the prostitute*."

American culture, entertainment, and American-produced internet made pornography ubiquitous. It was everywhere. Americans no longer had to go into the red-light district of American cities and towns to obtain pornographic materials. American culture had now become a red-light district.

Ishtar had triumphed. Her effect on America was so great that it had now become the world's leading creator and exporter of pornography. America was now, in fact, producing the *majority* of the world's pornographic content. It had become the undisputed porn capital of the world.

The civilization that had been consecrated at its inception to advancing the gospel and spreading the light of God to the nations was covering the earth with pornography and advancing the agenda of another spirit, that which now controlled it—that of the prostitute goddess.

—————◆◆◆—————

What do sex, drugs, and rock and roll, fortune-tellers and witchcraft, intoxication, New Age movements, and the world of the occult have to do with one another?

They all go back to the enchantments of a Mesopotamian goddess.

Chapter 21

The Intoxicator

A S AN ENCHANTRESS, Ishtar tempted, allured, and captivated. She caused her followers to abandon reason and rationality to do what they otherwise would never have done. She cast spells. She worked magic. Thus her ability to seduce was all the more potent.

Ishtar's Potion

As the goddess who dwelled in taverns, Ishtar was strongly connected to the substances of intoxication served and partaken of there. In one of her myths she schemes to take away the powers and blueprints of civilization contained in the tablets of the god Enki. She partakes with him of alcoholic beverages until he becomes intoxicated, at which point she takes off with the tablets.

So to Ishtar belonged the powers of both seduction and intoxication. Thus it is of note that at the same time that the sexual revolution was taking hold of America, a parallel movement began, an explosion in the usage of intoxicating substances.

After holding steady from the end of the Second World War, the rate of American alcohol consumption suddenly began rising. The escalation would continue for two decades and then would be followed by another escalation that would continue into the twenty-first century.

The Mind Alterer

But it was another form of intoxication that so dramatically exploded in American and Western culture that it would, in part, define the 1960s: that of drugs. The phenomenon became so widespread that it gave birth to its own culture—the drug culture.

Among the most celebrated of the newly embraced intoxicating substances were the psychedelic, or "mind-altering," drugs that radically altered perception, thinking, and behavior. The state of intoxication and altered consciousness was now glorified as an ideal to be sought after.

It was all in keeping with the goddess's nature. It was her power and will to alter consciousness, perception, and reality. With or without intoxicating substances she was altering the American consciousness.

89

Sex, Drugs, Rock, and Ishtar

For the ancient Mesopotamian, the taverns were inhabited by the spirit of Ishtar. It was there that those affected by her allurements were surrounded by three elements: sexuality, intoxicating substances, and music. When the spirit of Ishtar manifested in American culture in the 1960s, two of the three elements also manifested, sexuality and intoxicating substances. The third component would converge as well—music.

Each of the three would epitomize the decade that began the transformation of American culture. In 1969 a *LIFE* magazine article identified the three elements as the counterculture's new sacraments—"*sex, drugs and rock*,"[1] or sexuality, intoxicating substances, and music—the three elements that characterized Ishtar's dwelling place.

Medium of the Gods

The Mesopotamians especially sought the power of Ishtar in performing magic and enchantments on those in their lives. She was the goddess of spells. Her powers were called upon to redirect or inflame a person's sexual desire or romantic affection. The spell could involve rituals, the use of objects, apples, pomegranates, the weaving together of cords into knots, symbolic acts that today would be called sympathetic magic or witchcraft.

Ishtar was the goddess of mediums, those who were said to be possessed of the spirits. They spoke for the gods and revealed supernatural knowledge and counsel. Her spirit possessed them, as it did her prophets. Ishtar herself was a medium, the mediator between the gods and mortals. Today, such mediums would also be known as fortune-tellers, psychics, channelers, and practitioners of the occult. Indeed, all these elements associated with the goddess would today be categorized under the heading of the occult. She was the occult goddess.

The Occult Revival

Thus we might expect that with the return of Ishtar to the modern world, there would be a revival in the occult. And that, again, is exactly what happened. It was no accident that the same decade that witnessed America's turning from God, the beginning of the sexual revolution, the overturning of gender, the weakening of family, and the wide dissemination of mind-altering substances also witnessed a massive revival in the occult. The spiritual void left in God's absence drew millions into a dark spirituality. And as with other movements launched by the gods, occult beliefs and practices moved from the fringes and shadows of society to its mainstream.

Witches and Goddesses

Out of the occult revival came an explosion in the practice of witchcraft as well as in the number of women identifying as witches. In this they were taking on the attributes of the goddess. The occult revival would also give birth to the revival of pagan worship, neo-pagan movements, and hybrid movements that merged the occult with Eastern religions and ancient paganism. It would also produce movements, organizations, and religions dedicated to Satan worship.

There was one other movement of special note that would also spring up from the seeds planted in the late-twentieth-century occult revival— goddess worship. It was an outgrowth of the neo-pagan movements born of that revival. It included the worship of mother goddesses, nature goddesses, warrior goddesses, and "great goddesses," among others. Often included in the pantheon of goddesses to be venerated or worshipped was the goddess in her varied incarnations of Astarte, Aphrodite, Venus, Inanna, and, of course, Ishtar.

The Grand Enchantment

The revival of goddess worship was also an outgrowth of the feminist revival that happened simultaneously to the occult revival. Both were linked to Ishtar. Now the two converged. But it was all converging: the sexual revolution with feminism, feminism with the occult, the occult with intoxicating substances, intoxicating substances with music, and music with the sexual revolution. In the goddess they were all joined together.

They were all joined together as well in that they were part of the paganization of America and the re-paganization of Western civilization. As we have seen, the *"new morality"* was a revival of pagan morality, the occult and New Age beliefs were a revival of pagan rituals and religious practices, and the sexual revolution was a reviving of pagan sexuality.

The gods were succeeding in transforming a Christian civilization into a pagan one. Transformation was Ishtar's specialty. She could enchant and seduce a nation, intoxicate it, alter its perceptions, and thus change its ways, entrance it, and possess it.

What began taking hold of American and Western civilization in the 1960s would continue unfolding, developing, and advancing long after the decade had come to an end.

◆◆◆

But there was still one more player in the dark trinity. It could be argued that this was the darkest of the three. It is to that spirit and mystery that we go now—the third of the dark trinity—that of the Destroyer.

Part VI:

THE

DESTROYER

Chapter 22

The Destroyer

H E WAS THE most mysterious of the dark trinity. There is, to this day, debate over who exactly he was. His identity belonged to the shadows. But the evil he represented could not be more stark or brazen. He was Molech.

The Abomination God

His name makes several appearances in Scripture. When King Solomon fell away from God, he built high places, altars and sanctuaries for the foreign gods. One of them was Molech:

> Then Solomon built a high place for Chemosh the
> abomination of Moab, on the hill that is east of Jerusalem,
> and for Molech the abomination of the people of Ammon.[1]

So horrifying was the nature of the god and his worship that he is called *"the abomination."* The earliest of scriptural mentions warns of the evil associated with that name:

> And you shall not let any of your descendants pass
> through the fire to Molech.[2]

When the righteous king Josiah endeavored to lead his nation back to God, he knew he had to destroy the altars of Molech:

> And he defiled Topheth, which is in the Valley of the Son
> of Hinnom, that no man might make his son or his
> daughter pass through the fire to Molech.[3]

Molech was associated with the darkest of sins—the sacrifice of human beings and, in particular, the sacrifice of children. Even darker, Molech is associated with the sacrifice of children by their parents. The Bible speaks of the act as the most grievous of *"abominations"* as well as the sign of a nation that has turned entirely against the ways of God and become lost to Him.

The God and the Sacrifice

The name Molech can be translated as "king." A number of modern scholars have theorized that the word *Molech* should rather be translated as a verb denoting the act of child sacrifice itself rather than a god. But verses such as Leviticus 20:5, which reads in the original Hebrew as "*liznote aharei ha Molekh*," or "*who prostitute themselves with the Molech*," and others would argue against that. And to every sacrifice there is a god. So there would still remain a god to whom the child sacrifices spoken of in Scripture were offered. Some theorize that Molech was another form of Baal since he too is spoken of as receiving children as sacrifices. But even if there was anything to any of those theories, the act and practice of sacrificing children is of a demonic realm so uniquely of its own category and nature that the name Molech stands uniquely on its own.

The Horror of the Name

Beyond that we must keep in mind the nature of the beast. The relationship between the gods and spirits is symbiotic. The mythologies and beliefs of men may follow after the principalities and spirits—and the principalities and spirits may follow after the mythologies and beliefs of men. In that sense the argument becomes immaterial.

Molech is the spirit and god of child sacrifice. It is the principality of bloodlust, of cold, inhuman, and horrid destruction.

In his epic poem *Paradise Lost*, John Milton writes of the ancient god:

> First Moloch, horrid King besmeared with blood
> Of human sacrifice, and parents' tears,
> Though for the noise of drums and timbrels loud
> Their children's cries unheard, that pass'd through fire
> To his grim idol.[4]

In the twentieth century Winston Churchill used the figure of Molech to speak of the evil of Adolf Hitler:

> He had conjured up the fearful idol of an all-devouring
> Moloch of which he was the priest and incarnation.[5]

The name of the ancient god has retained its horror down through the ages.

His Molten Hands

Do we have any idea what the worship of Molech was like? The Bible cites Israel's ancient neighbors, the Canaanites, as those who participated in child sacrifice. The ancient Greek and Roman historians bear witness to the biblical testimony as they record the practices of two Canaanite people in particular, the Phoenicians and those of their African colony, Carthage. The ancient Greek historian Diodorus Siculus records this of the Carthaginians:

> There was in their city a bronze image of Cronus, extending
> its hands, palms up and sloping toward the ground, so that
> each of the children when placed thereon rolled down and
> fell into a sort of gaping pit filled with fire.[6]

Cronus was the Greek version of the Roman Saturn, the god who devoured his own children. His name is used either because the Carthaginians had now associated him with Molech or Baal or because this was how Diodorus had made sense of what was taking place.

The Darkest Depths

Child sacrifice was part of the rites and worship of the pagan peoples and cultures that surrounded the Israelites. So when the Israelites turned away from God, they turned to the ways of the gods—they began offering up their children. The prophet Jeremiah would confront the depths of their fall from God and the gruesome sin they were now partaking in and celebrating:

> And they built the high places of Baal which are in the
> Valley of the Son of Hinnom, to cause their sons and their
> daughters to pass through the fire to Molech.[7]

It was the deepest and darkest of depths of their fall from God.

◆◆◆

But what if such practices were much more common than we would imagine?

What if it was the prohibition of such practices rather than the practices themselves that was the exception to the rule?

What part do the gods and spirits have in such practices?

And what if those gods, or one god in particular, was to come back?

The Abominable Sacrifice

How could anything so gruesome as child sacrifice, so morally abhorrent, and so obviously contrary to all that undergirds human existence be embraced and practiced by any people or nation?

The Most Pagan of Acts

In the case of the pagan world, it was the result of God's absence. In the case of Israel, it was the result of turning from God's presence. And yet, contrary to what we might expect, the practice was not unique or exceptional. Rather, it was nearly universal. It could be found in the temples of ancient Egypt to the shrines of Tahiti, from the altars of Mesopotamia to the hanging trees of Germany, from India to Hawaii, from West Africa to Tibet, from the Aztecs to the Celts, from the Druids to the Mongolians, and among countless other peoples in countless other lands.

Human and child sacrifice were symptomatic of pagan culture, thought, and values, and the overall devaluation and degradation of life. Beyond sacrifice, the young were especially vulnerable in pagan culture to mistreatment, abuse, and murder. Infants with deformities or disabilities were commonly discarded by their parents, left in garbage dumps, drowned in rivers, exposed to the elements, or abandoned to wild animals.

The Disposable Life

Even children born perfectly healthy could be murdered if, for some reason, they were not found desirable or wanted by their parents. And even some of the most revered philosophers and esteemed leaders of the ancient world could endorse or decree the death of innocent children. It was not safe to be a child in the ancient pagan world. One could be murdered at the moment of one's birth, or before or after. It was not at all uncommon for children to be killed in their mothers' wombs. With the pagan devaluation of human life came a bent toward death—the spirit of Molech.

Therefore, when a nation or civilization turns away from God, we can expect the same values and horrors to be revived. It is no accident that the same nation that turned from Christian faith and replaced biblical values with pagan ones, Nazi Germany, came to view the sickly and weak as contemptible and disposable, then set out to exterminate them. So too when the Soviet government purged biblical values from Russia, human life, likewise, became disposable. In each case, the departure from biblical values to pagan or neo-pagan values resulted in the murder of millions.

When I Was Made in Secret

The biblical view of life, children, and the weak could not have been more different than that of the pagan world. From the very opening chapters of the Bible it was established that human life was created in the image of God. Thus every human life, whether young or old, male or female, strong or weak, rich or poor, healthy or infirm, was of infinite value. The idea of slaughtering one's children on the altars of the gods was forbidden, abhorrent, and an abomination. The Lord was said to have carried Israel *"as a man carries his son."*[1] Children were now to be viewed as *"a gift from the Lord."*[2] They were thus to be cherished and treasured.

Life was to be treated as precious and sacred from the moment of conception. So in the psalms King David could write:

> You formed my inward parts; You covered me in my mother's womb....My frame was not hidden from You, when I was made in secret....And in Your book they all were written, the days fashioned for me, when as yet there were none of them.[3]

For Such Is the Kingdom

In the New Testament the status of the weak, the infirm, or the defenseless was further elevated. Jesus comforted the weak, embraced the outcast, and healed the sick. As for children, their value was elevated to a level previously unknown in human history. He said this:

> Let the little children come to Me, and do not forbid them; for of such is the kingdom of heaven.[4]

And again:

> I say to you, unless you...become as little children, you will by no means enter the kingdom of heaven. Therefore whoever humbles himself as this little child is the greatest

in the kingdom of heaven. Whoever receives one little child like this in My name receives Me.[5]

The Teachings of Your Gods

So with the entrance of the gospel into the pagan world, there came an inevitable collision of values over the sanctity of human life, the value of women, the treatment of the weak, the care of the sick, and the worth and protection of children, born and unborn.

Wherever human sacrifice was performed, the ascendancy of the gospel would bring the practice to an end. In the case of the Roman Empire, it was the Christian faith that caused the practice of infanticide, the killing of little children, to disappear. As to the killing of unborn children, though restrictions had, at times, been enacted over the issue of parental rights, the act was widely accepted and practiced. But with the coming of the gospel, the practice of killing children, born or unborn, was challenged. The early Christian writer Lactantius wrote this of the pagan world's murder of its children:

> They either strangle the sons born from themselves, or if they are too "pious," they expose them....Can those persons be considered innocent who expose their own offspring as prey for dogs?[6]

And the early Christian apologist Marcus Minucius Felix wrote of the link of abortion and the pagan gods:

> So they commit murder before they bring forth. And these things assuredly *come down from the teaching of your gods.*[7]

The murder of little children came down from the teachings of their gods.

If Molech Returned

It was the Christian faith and the biblical valuing of human life that brought protection to young and unborn children and the definitive end of their large-scale murder.

So when the gods were cast out of Western civilization, a spirit of death went with them. The gospel had removed their altars and the blood that had stained them. As the gods departed, lives were saved. Prisoners, slaves, and little children were now spared from being slaughtered as human sacrifices. Countless others were saved from being murdered outright or left out to die in the wilderness as babies. And still others were saved from being killed in their mothers' wombs.

The gods of death were sent into exile. Among them was Molech. But if the gods and spirits departed as the civilizations they had once possessed had turned to God, what would then happen if those same civilizations should turn away from God? The gods of death would return.

Then Molech would return.

◆◆◆

And if Molech returned, would he not again require blood and human sacrifice?

And according to the parable, would not his latter work be worse than his first?

And if the ancient Destroyer returned, what would happen to the children?

Chapter 24

The Destroyer Returns

HOW DID THE most ominous god of the dark trinity return?

The mystery would provide us with a clue—not only as to how he would return, but when.

Molech in the Soviet Union

The end of child and human sacrifice was replayed in every land where the Christian faith prevailed. But if those nations and civilizations should turn from that faith, what would happen? The dark principalities would return, the ancient blood fury would be revived, and the slaughter of the innocents would begin anew.

It is no accident that after renouncing Christianity, that which would soon be known as the Soviet Union became the first state to legalize the killing of unborn children. It did so in 1920, soon after coming to power, with its legalization of abortion. Years later, out of concerns for population growth, the law would be temporarily reversed, before being restored again. It is revealing that it was the *godless* and anti-Christian Soviet Union that was first in the modern world to revive the ancient horror.

Molech in Nazi Germany

In the case of the other demonically anti-Christian power of the twentieth century, Nazi Germany, the issue of child sacrifice is more complex. The Third Reich was first concerned with the conquest and proliferation of the *"master race."* Therefore, it was opposed to abortions as much as they affected German or Aryan birth rates. But the Nazis were servants of the gods and ministers of human sacrifice. The blood fury came out in their obsession with slaughtering the sons and daughters of others.

Molech was especially interested in Jewish children. In ancient times he had killed thousands of them. Now his spirit would cause one and a half million of them to perish.

The Third God

But as far as a large-scale reentrance of Molech into Western civilization and the world, that would require a massive and civilizational turning from God. Again, we are brought back to the pivotal decade of the 1960s. We saw first the entrance and workings of Baal, then of Ishtar. Now must come Molech, the third of the dark trinity and the principality of death.

We would expect, as in ancient times, the spirit of Molech to set its gaze on little children, the infants that had once been laid on its molten hands. We would expect that it would require their blood and demand their lives. And we would expect its appearance to follow in the wake of the first two gods and thus in the latter part of that decade or the early part of the next. And that is exactly what happened.

And so it began in the late 1960s, when a handful of American states opened the door by legalizing the killing of unborn children. Then, on January 22, 1973, the Supreme Court legalized the murder of unborn children. Molech had come to America.

Baal to Molech

He had help. The gods of the dark trinity had worked together. Without Baal laying the groundwork, moving the nation away from its biblical foundation, the idea of taking a human life in the image of God would have been unthinkable. But that foundation had been broken. So too the pagan blurring of distinctions, as in the bull-horned images of Baal, had weakened the line between human and animal. And while it, perhaps, elevated animal life, human life was devalued.

Further, the idolatry that came with Baal, in which one could forge one's own idol, create one's own god, and fashion one's own truth and values, meant that there was no more truth or absolutes. Each could do as he or she pleased. And if one could create one's own truth, one now could destroy the truth that actually existed, as in a human life, the unborn child.

Ishtar to Molech

Baal ushered in Ishtar. And it was Ishtar who ushered in Molech. Her mythologies were filled with unrestrained sexuality yet with no apparent thought of, desire for, or connection to children. Her indulgences led not to life but death.

Beyond that was the goddess's deeper work. Her sexual revolution had severed sexuality from marriage, husbands from wives, men from fatherhood, and women from motherhood. The most critical bond of life, that of mother and child, had eroded. The natural maternal instinct to save one's child at all costs was weakened and, in some cases, gone. And so as in ancient times little children were now brought by their mothers to the altars of Molech.

The Gifts of Ishtar

It is believed that in ancient times the cult of Ashtoreth, or Ishtar, worked in tandem with the cults of Baal and Molech and the gods of child sacrifice. Children produced by sexual acts in the temples or by Ishtar's prostitutes on the streets provided sacrifices for the gods. So now in modern times, as the sexual revolution bore its fruit, more and more children were conceived outside of marriage and were more likely to be unwanted. Their lives would provide the modern-day sacrifices of Molech.

The City on the Hill of Molech

America was now offering up its own children as sacrifices. Other nations would be led by its example into taking up the gruesome practice as well. Millions of unborn children around the world would now perish in Molech's shadow.

God had warned Israel that if it turned against His ways, if it turned to the gods, it would end up sacrificing its own children. And so it had. And now so too had America. And so too had the nations of the West. And all these had influenced the rest of the world.

It was one more step of re-paganization, one more piece of the ancient pagan world returning to the modern. The civilization that had, in ancient times, cast out the spirits was now repossessed by them, and America, the shining *city on the hill*, had now become a blood-soaked high place of Molech.

————◆◆◆————

Could one of the most widespread and controversial of practices in American culture go back to the rites of the ancient Canaanites?

And could the ancient accounts of those rites give us revelation as to what is taking place in our midst?

Chapter 25

Children of the Altars

WHAT WAS IT that could cause a mother of ancient times to lift the child of her womb to Molech?

The Molech Keys to Success

For one thing, she believed that by so doing, she would obtain the god's favor. Her fields would be fruitful. She would be given prosperity. Her prayers would be given answers. And her life would be blessed.

The Greek writer Cleitarchus is credited with this report connecting child sacrifice and gain:

> Out of reverence for Kronos, the Phoenicians, and especially the Carthaginians, whenever they seek to obtain some great favour, vow one of their children, burning it as a sacrifice to the deity, if they are especially eager to gain success.[1]

So in the modern replaying, what could lead a mother to kill the son or daughter of her womb? The most frequently given answer is that if the child lived, it would hamper the mother's life, her time, her energy, her educational or career prospects, her future earning capabilities. The child would be a burden to her aspirations. Thus by killing the child, the hindrance and burden would be removed and she would be in a better position to achieve her goals and attain success and prosperity.

Female celebrities, feminist leaders, and other women of influence would publicly boast that they were able to find success in their careers because they ended the lives of their unborn children. Thus the reason given was, in essence, the same as that which led the ancient mothers to lift their children onto Molech's altars. By doing so, they believed they were invoking blessing, prosperity, and gain. It is hard to fathom how anyone, ancient or modern, could make such a decision, but the decision remained unchanged.

Can a Woman Forget?

In the ancient sacrifice of Molech, the mother or father would bring the child to the altar to be slaughtered. So it is a unique dynamic of abortion that it is the mother or father who presents the child to be killed.

In the Book of Isaiah the voice of God asks this question:

> Can a woman forget her nursing child, and not have compassion on the son of her womb? Surely they may forget, yet I will not forget you.[2]

In the case of Molech and in the case of abortion, the answer is yes. Even mothers may forget. How could something as intrinsic to life as a mother's instinct to protect her child morph into the desire to kill her child? Such things, ancient or modern, are not natural. They are the works of the gods.

In the ancient sacrifice the parent would either kill or else present the child to the priest or officiant, who would then take its life. In the modern sacrifice the mother, in effect, gives her baby to the officiant, the abortionist, who then takes its life.

In the ancient sacrifice the child could be pierced, cut, crushed, left to die, and/or burned. Burning was so common a feature that the Scriptures rebuke the Israelites for causing their children to *pass through the fire.* In the modern sacrifice the child was likewise pierced, cut, torn apart, left to die, or, through the use of chemical solutions—burned.

Music to Kill By

The Greek philosopher Plutarch describes the music that would accompany the sacrifices of children and its purpose:

> "...and the whole area before the statue was filled with a
> loud noise of flutes and drums so that the cries of wailing
> should not reach the ears of the people.[3]

In one sense the music represented a civilization's celebration of child sacrifice. So too, under the spell of Molech, we have seen not only the return of child sacrifice but a civilization's celebration of the act.

But according to Plutarch, the music was especially strategic.

The horror of the act was so intense that the public was kept shielded from hearing it by the sound of flutes and drums. So too in its modern replaying, the horror of putting a baby to death in abortion was so disturbing that its sights, sounds, and details were kept hidden from the public. And the baby's agony could only be expressed in the form of silent screams that no one would hear.

The Racist God

Diodorus Siculus writes of a secret transaction concerning the child sacrifices of his day:

> They had been accustomed to sacrifice to this god the noblest of their sons, but more recently, secretly buying and nurturing children, they had sent these to the sacrifice.[4]

In other words, the rich were buying children from those who were not rich, in order to sacrifice them in place of their children. Plutarch writes of similar transactions:

> ...and those who had no children would buy little ones from poor people and cut their throats as if they were so many lambs or young birds; meanwhile the mother stood by without a tear or moan.[5]

So it was poor children who were more adversely affected by the child sacrifice than the rich. It was poor mothers who were more likely to offer up their children. And far more of poor children than the rich were placed on the altar.

Even this was replayed in the modern version of child sacrifice. Abortion was weighted against the children of the poor and of minorities. The child of a poor family and particularly of a Black family was far more likely to be killed by abortion than the child who was not Black or poor. And there were now American cities where more Black children were killed through abortion than were actually born. It was one of Molech's many evils that he hated the poor and downcast and was a racist.

A Culture of Cannibals

In the pagan world it was believed that child sacrifice resulted in benefits not only for the individual who offered it but to the entire society. It would bring the god's favor and enhance the public good. If a misfortune or calamity came upon the land, it could result in the sacrificing of multitudes of children to appease the god and bring relief to the land. So the Roman philosopher Porphyry writes:

> The Phoenicians too, in great disasters whether of wars, or droughts, or plagues, used to sacrifice one of their dearest, dedicating him to Kronos.[6]

So the modern practice of child sacrifice was likewise hailed for its beneficial effect on the "public good." The killing of babies was said to benefit society not only in freeing women to pursue careers but for holding the promise of breakthroughs in medicine and health. To further enhance this "public good," and to increase their profit margin, the abortion industry engaged in the sale of baby parts harvested from the murdered children. The spirit of Molech, having mixed children's blood with profit, had created a culture of cannibals.

Molech's Priests

The Greek philosopher Plato wrote of how the Carthaginian culture viewed child sacrifice:

> With us, for instance, human sacrifice is not legal, but unholy, whereas the Carthaginians perform it as a thing they account *holy* and legal.[7]

So the Carthaginians not only legalized the practice; they deemed it as *holy*. Even this ancient dynamic was replayed in America and the modern world. The killing of an unborn child was not only legal but was hallowed as a *sacred* right to be praised, celebrated, and venerated as something beautiful and sacrosanct.

In ancient Israel it was the priests of Molech and Baal who would hallow the murder of children by speaking of it in religious terms. Who, then, are the modern-day priests of Molech? They are the ones who perform the act and those who sanctify it, the corporations that profit from children's blood, the political leaders and legislators who fight to ensure that Molech's temples remain overflowing with offerings, and the radical activists and ideologues who speak blessings and praises over the savage act as they lead women to the altars.

Blessings and Sacraments

The following are some of the actual words spoken by those who sanctify the killing of unborn children. Notice the framing of the act in religious and spiritual terms—as well as the word *sacrifice*:

> Our culture needs new *rituals* as well as laws to *restore abortion* to its *sacred* dimension.[8]

> Abortion [is] a major *blessing*, and...a *sacrament* in the hands of women.[9]

> It is not immoral to choose abortion; it is simply another kind of morality, *a pagan one*.[10]

> Abortion is a *sacrifice*.[11]

> Abortion is a *sacred act*.[12]

There is nothing else needing to be written here. Nothing could in any way add to or take away from the significance or horror of such words.

◆◆◆

There was a specific place in ancient Israel where the mystery of Molech was centered and came to its most dramatic conclusion. It would usher in the nation's judgment.

Does it have a modern parallel? And does it contain a warning for another civilization and another nation?

Chapter 26

The Valley of Hinnom

THE PROPHET LOOKED out into the valley where the Lord had sent him. It was the site of the nation's darkest of sins. He had been told to go there to deliver a prophecy of judgment:

> Because they have forsaken Me and made this an alien place, because they have burned incense in it to other gods whom neither they, their fathers, nor the kings of Judah have known, *and have filled this place with the blood of the innocents.*[1]

Ashes, Bones, and Blood

It was the Valley of Hinnom, the ground that bore witness to the depths to which the nation had descended in its fall from God. It was filled with blood, ashes, and little bones, the evidence of murder. The people had come to that valley to worship their new gods and *"burn their sons and their daughters in the fire."*[2]

The prophet was Jeremiah, known as *"the weeping prophet,"* for the tears he shed over his nation's fall. It was beyond his fathoming how a nation so blessed, so favored with promise, and so filled with the revelation of God could descend to the horrors in the Valley of Hinnom. But the gods had accomplished it.

Their aim, from the beginning, was revealed in the end, in the Valley of Hinnom. The goal was destruction—of the nation's children and of the nation itself. The gods had caused mothers to forget their motherhood and lift up their babies to the molten god that would destroy them. The gods had deafened the nation to the screaming of their little children on the altars in the valley.

Millions on the Altars

America had its own Valley of Hinnom. It was every place in which the nation's unwanted children were put to death. Israel had killed thousands of its sons and daughters. America had killed millions. From the time that their murder was legalized in the early 1970s, America had spilled the blood of approximately one million children every year. By the second decade of the twenty-first century, it had killed over sixty million of them. It was a Valley of Hinnom of unfathomable proportions, of endless blood, ashes, and little bones.

How could it have happened? How could a nation that once prided itself in being Christian, under God, and the moral beacon of the world have fallen into such depths of evil?

Their Blood Crying Out

It happened just as it had to ancient Israel, in a progression of seduction. The spirit of Baal had caused America to believe that departing from God would bring it freedom. The spirit of Ishtar had convinced it that if it abandoned its moral safeguards for instant gratification and sexual abandon, it would find fulfillment. And the spirit of Molech had promised to grant it the blessings of an unhindered life if it would only allow him to take away its children.

Baal, Ishtar, and Molech, the dark trinity of Israel's fall, had again seduced a nation and an entire civilization. The promise of their seduction would remain unmet. It would lead instead to a state of brokenness, emptiness, and now death.

The paganization of America and Western civilization was now reaping its most bloody of fruits. The once Christian civilization was now taking part in the most pagan of acts—the killing of its own children, their blood crying out to heaven.

The Soviet Union, Nazi Germany, America

When Germany turned away from God and the Christian faith, the powers of hell were unleashed. The result was the murder of six million Jews and a world war that would see the perishing of tens of millions. When Russia morphed into the Soviet Union and turned away from God and the Christian faith, the result was, again, the murder of tens of millions of people. When America began turning away from God and the Christian faith, the result was the murder of over sixty million children. The removing of God and, in particular, the Christian faith is a most dangerous thing.

The murder of sixty million American children far exceeded anything Molech had accomplished in ancient times. But the parable said that when the spirits return to the house, they come back over seven times worse than at the start.

And Molech's death toll in the modern world would be greater still. America's welcoming in of Molech would ultimately lead other nations to do the same. Taking into account these other sacrifices of Molech, the killing of unborn children all over the world, the number of those murdered on his altars, the fruit of a world turned away from God, would far exceed one billion.

A Warning From Hinnom

The prophet Jeremiah warned Israel as to what would happen to a nation that had once known God and now lifts up its children as offerings to the gods. The end is destruction. There are few things that so invoke the judgment of God as the killing of little children.

The words of the prophet would now warn a civilization that had also once known God and was now offering up its children. The blood of millions now covered America's collective hands. It had departed from God and was now standing in the Valley of Hinnom, with ashes, bones, and blood—the blood crying out to heaven and likewise in danger of judgment.

◆◆◆

We are now about to open up the realm of the mystery that will touch upon the highest altars of American and Western civilization. It will now involve the most hallowed of modern sacred cows and idols. Thus it will become even more intense and more explosive.

We will now illuminate the most controversial of modern-day issues with the light of an ancient mystery. The illumination will involve avatars, modern-day priesthoods, and the playing out of ancient mythology in our midst and in real time.

We begin with the opening up of the mystery of the Transformer.

Part VII:

THE

TRANSFORMER

Chapter 27

The Transformer

T HERE WAS ANOTHER side to Ishtar, another nature, another power, and another agenda. And it would be from this, her other side, that the transformation of American and world culture would be taken to a new stage and a new level. And from this, new movements would spring forth that would alter the face of Western civilization beyond recognition.

We will now remove a veil to uncover an ancient mystery that lies behind the forces, movements, events, and phenomena that are at this moment touching and transforming virtually every facet of modern culture. And yet the mystery goes back thousands of years to the clay tablets of ancient Sumer.

Something About Ishtar

Ishtar was a sorceress. She was known for her powers to alter people's affections, passions, thoughts, and, at times, their essence. We are now about to see how, as a sorceress, she would alter more than human relationships and institutions in the modern world—something even deeper.

If the sexual revolution was the first of her renewed works, this would be her second. The second, though connected to the first, would open up a different realm. It would alter human desire, human identity, and human nature itself.

The transformation would follow after the goddess's own nature. There was something different about Ishtar.

I Am a Woman—I Am a Man

In her link to the planet Venus, she was known as the morning star but also the evening star. In this was a clue into her nature—duality. She would inhabit the two ends and polar opposites of the spectrum.

She was, on one hand, the goddess of love, beauty, allurement, and female sexuality. But on the other, she embodied and personified ferocity, aggressiveness, violence, battle, war, and destruction—characteristics and elements typically associated with masculinity. On one hand, she was shown as a naked woman in jewels, the goddess of sexuality, but on the other, an armored fighter, a symbol of war. She was, in one entity, the embodiment of male and female.

Ishtar's connection to both femininity and masculinity was more than allusion or metaphor. An ancient Mesopotamian tablet records the goddess saying these words:

> When I sit in the alehouse, I am a woman, and I am an exuberant young man.[1]

Another ancient writing records her saying this:

> Though I am a woman I am a noble young man.[2]

The core and operative words in such statements are these:

> I am a woman. I am a man.

To Turn a Man Into a Woman

The joining of the masculine and feminine in one being was, in many ways, what Ishtar was all about. It was her nature to cross lines, transgress boundaries, break conventions, blur distinctions, and merge opposites, to confuse and invert.

It was not her nature to accept reality as it was. It was her nature to bend it, transform it, conform it to her will and desire. If her will was to be a woman, she would be a woman. But if it was to be a man, she would become a man. She was the goddess of transmutation and metamorphosis.

Her nature was to alter nature and most specifically the nature of male and female, man and woman. An ancient Sumerian hymn reveals her power. It was to

> ...turn a man into a woman and a woman into a man, to change one into the other...[3]

She had the ability to turn male into female and female into male, to blur and bend and merge and invert the two.

The Transformer Returns

So what would happen if the goddess and that power came into the modern world? What would happen is what has already happened and is now happening.

It would mean that there would be another transformation, a deeper and further work. And because of that we would not expect it to dramatically manifest at the beginning of the sexual revolution but later on. And so it would. It would take the sexual revolution to a deeper stage, to its logical conclusions, and to another realm.

It would appear as something new, a new movement, a new dynamic to penetrate and transform American and Western culture. But behind it all was an ancient principality that was said to possess the power to transform human nature and reality.

The Transformer's Blueprint

Upon its return to the world, the ancient spirit would set out to accomplish its mission.

It would seek to alter the definition of *male* and *female*.

It would move to blur the lines and nullify the distinctions between the two.

It would act to transform the nature of man and woman.

It would seek to feminize all that was male and masculinize all that was female.

It would attempt to turn man into woman and woman into man.

It would war against the sanctity of sexuality and gender by confusing the two and merging the one into the other and the other into the one and, by so doing, seek to nullify them.

It would appear first at the fringes of society, where Ishtar was known to have dwelled. But then it would come into the mainstream and begin permeating every part of culture, leaving almost no facet of life untouched.

It would usher in the next stage of America's paganization. And it would become the chief hammerhead to smash the biblical foundations of Western civilization.

———————◆◆◆———————

We will now open up the goddess's deeper work and her darker magic. We will see how she cast her spell and altered a civilization and human nature.

It would begin with the spell she cast and the transformation she set in motion concerning *"her own kind"*—the metamorphosis of women.

Chapter 28

The Metamorphosis of Women

THE GODDESS WOULD inaugurate the metamorphosis and deconstruction of women.

The Masculine Goddess

It came from her own nature. Though some of her qualities were linked to femininity, especially in the sexual realm, other traditionally feminine qualities were missing, particularly that linked to nurturing—empathy, gentleness, compassion. They seemed foreign to her. She was not a caregiver, and there was almost nothing maternal about her.

Her temperament was, in many ways, more characterized by attributes commonly associated with masculinity. She was a fighter. She was assertive, aggressive, dominant, combative, competitive, courageous, fierce, strong, independent, violent, brave, and ferocious. And it was her nature and power to make others into her image—and thus to turn *"a woman into a man."*

The Masculinization of Women

So we would expect, then, that as the spirit of Ishtar took hold of American and Western culture, there would begin a transformation of women, a morphing of their identities, functioning, and nature. And that is exactly what happened. The goddess would seek to defeminize women, to masculinize them to share in her nature. To do that, she would have to destroy or weaken the male-female paradigm. She would have to separate woman from man and man from woman.

Ishtar in the Workplace

Ishtar has been referred to as an "independent woman" due to the fact that, in the end, she was never bound to any one man, and as one associated with prostitution, she was economically self-supporting.[1] So at the same time the sexual revolution was taking hold, there was a growing movement calling for women to become, like Ishtar, economically independent of men.

Millions of women left their homes to join the workforce. The decline of marriage only furthered the trend. Divorce had increased the number of women without husbands, many of them single mothers. They now had to replace the functions of the missing husband and take on the traditionally male roles of provider and protector. Women were increasingly told to seek meaning and fulfillment not in marriage or motherhood or family but in the workforce.

Transformed Into Her Image

But function and role affect identity and even nature. The identity and nature of women began changing. Women were encouraged and instructed to become aggressive, competitive, dominant, and fierce. Girls were now trained from early childhood to reject typically feminine pursuits. They were bombarded with messages about "girl power" and fierceness, just as the goddess was fierce and powerful. As Ishtar took on masculine roles and characteristics, so women were impelled to do likewise, to assume traditional masculine functions, work, attributes, and roles. The new zeitgeist, or spirit, of the age belonged to Ishtar. And it was causing women, step by step, to be transformed into her image.

Rage of the Goddess

Ishtar was bent on breaking conventions. She eschewed traditionally feminine roles and instead competed with men, fighting with them, defying them, and dominating them. So at the same time the spirit of Ishtar was setting in motion the sexual revolution, another movement was birthed, *feminism*, or *"second-wave feminism."* It would be infused from its beginning with the spirit of the goddess. It would thus also set out to break societal conventions, wage war against the concept of femininity, and defy male authority. As Ishtar was given to rage, so a spirit of rage against men became prevalent in American and Western culture, especially within the ranks of radical feminism.

Against the Patriarchy

The god Anu was the chief deity of the Mesopotamian pantheon. He was Ishtar's father. Ishtar would typically challenge his authority and seek to overrule it. The Latin word for father is *pater*. From *pater* we get the word *patriarchy*, or *"the ruling fathers."* So the spirit of Ishtar indwelling radical feminism set itself against what it called *the patriarchy*. The *patriarchy* had to be defied and overthrown.

Rise of the Warrior Women

But not only was Ishtar combative; she was a warrior. The Sumerian poem "Inana and Ebih" describes the goddess in her ferocity as she enters into battle:

> Goddess of the fearsome divine powers, clad in terror, riding on the great divine powers, Inana [*Ishtar*]... drenched in blood, rushing around in great battles... you destroy mighty lands with arrow and strength and overpower lands.[2]

Thus as the spirit of Ishtar began taking hold of American and Western culture, women now began taking on the identities and roles of fighters and warriors. The spirit of the military goddess was manifest in the militarization of women. It was what had been written in ancient times of the goddess's powers and acts. As is inscribed on the ancient tablets, she was at work to put

> ...spindles into the hands of men...and to *give weapons to the women*.[3]

So the warrior women became part of popular culture and entertainment where physical combat had once been the domain of men. Women were now increasingly depicted in fiction as bearing supernatural powers to war and wreak destruction. It was all in keeping with the mythology of the ancient warrior goddess.

The Militarized Goddess

Ishtar entered into the battlefield, fully armored and weaponed. It was in her nature, skill, and power to wage war. She was a militarized goddess. So upon her return, not only would she revive the image, fantasy, and narrative of the warrior goddess; she would bring about the militarization of women. In other words, the warrior woman would manifest as well in real life.

It was a phenomenon that was largely unprecedented for most of human history—the entering of women into military combat. The precedent, though, could be found in mythology. The goddess's myths were now becoming reality.

It was another manifestation of women being conformed into the goddess's image. And it was also another step in the divorcing of man and woman, male and female. The more women could resemble men or replicate their functions, the less they would need them. Women were now to be their own protectors and defenders. And so this too would feed into the goddess's destruction of marriage. The bond that held man and woman together was progressively deteriorating.

Whom Ishtar Deprived

It was no accident that marriage and family was being continually devalued, the workplace continually glorified, and sexual promiscuity or any sexuality devoid of marriage continually celebrated. Having been indoctrinated into the cult of self and self-fulfillment, both men and women were now more reluctant to enter into marriage and less able to maintain it. Both women and men were now more likely to end up alone. So an ancient Mesopotamian text speaks of the women

> *...whom Ishtar deprived of husbands...*[4]

Ishtar had promised the liberation of women. And yet studies into the state of women's well-being revealed that since the beginning of the transformation, they had, instead, grown progressively unhappier.[5] They were now less likely to be married, more likely to be in the workforce, less likely to be fulfilled, and more likely to be alone.

And yet even in this they had been unwittingly conformed to the image of the goddess.

———◆◆◆———

The goddess would not stop with women. If she was going to transform cultures, nations, and civilizations, she would have to transform men as well.

We now move to her other spell and the other transformation she began—the metamorphosis of men.

Chapter 29

The Metamorphosis of Men

AS SHE HAD done with women, Ishtar would inaugurate the metamorphosis and deconstruction of men.

The Emasculator

The goddess was never at ease with masculinity—if it was not her own, if it belonged to a man. Her lovers were dominated by her and tended to suffer a tragic fate. With regard to men, Ishtar was dangerous and deadly. She was their emasculator. A Hittite hymn to the goddess describes her as the one who will

> ...grind away from men manliness.[1]

Thus it was Ishtar's nature to remove manhood from men, to grind it away from them. In the original language, that which the goddess wrested from men was their *zikratu*. The word refers to potency, masculinity, and heroic power.

It was all part of her merging and confusing of gender. If one can remove masculinity from men, one can destroy the distinction between male and female. Then one can destroy marriage, the family, and then society.

It was Ishtar's power and desire to turn not only a woman into a man but "*a man into a woman.*"[2]

The Feminization of Men

So if the goddess's spirit was to begin permeating Western civilization, we would expect that civilization to begin warring against the masculinity of men. And that is exactly what happened. Male attributes as exhibited by men were increasingly attacked and deemed to be "*toxic masculinity.*" Men had to be demasculinized. An ancient prayer speaks of her power to emasculate men, to remove their ability to fight and protect. She would

> ...take away their swords, bows, arrows, daggers...then put into their hand the distaff and the mirror.[3]

With women increasingly taking on the roles of men, with marriage continuing to weaken, with more marriages ending in divorce and others never starting, men were increasingly separated from their traditional roles and functions of provider and protector. So as the roles and nature of women were being altered, so too were those of men.

She *took away their swords* and gave them *the distaff and the mirror.* So the spirit of the goddess would first seek to emasculate men, and then feminize them. And so as women were now instructed to show strength, men were now instructed to show weakness. It was the goddess's ancient magic.

Old Authorities and New Gods

For the transformation to be complete, the war against male leadership and authority could not be confined to any particular segment of society; it would have to pervade the entire culture. And so a spirit took hold of American and Western culture, a spirit that relentlessly attacked any association of men with leadership—whether in public life, popular culture, or the home.

Men were increasingly portrayed as being unable or unfit to lead, as either toxic oppressors or bumbling overgrown children. America went from the ethos of *Father Knows Best* to the depiction of fathers who knew almost nothing and served only as the objects of the jokes and mockery. The goddess was doing just as she had done in ancient times, challenging male leadership and demasculinizing men. As to Ishtar's corrosive effect on men, one scholar noted that it was her power and nature to

> ...destroy masculinity...effectively a destruction of the cultural order.[4]

If she could destroy masculinity, if she could delegitimize the authority of the father and of men in general, she could transform society. If the old leadership was nullified, then a culture could be led onto a different path. And if the old authority could be mocked and neutralized, then new authorities could take over—in this case, new gods.

The Reprogramming of Boys

And just as in the metamorphosis of women, the metamorphosis of men had to begin in childhood. While girls were told to be strong, boys were not. If boys displayed typical male characteristics, they would likely be reproved. They were less and less encouraged to succeed, and they began falling further and further behind in their education. Thus their likelihood of assuming positions of leadership in future days was deteriorating.

As for the natural male disposition to fight and protect, the impulse was now being channeled into video games. A generation of boys was now growing up addicted to computer screens. Their inclination to protect was thus being channeled away from marriage and family and into the universe of virtual reality.

As for sexuality, their desires were likewise now increasingly channeled away from reality and into the world of online pornography. The goddess was making sure from early on that the glue that had held together man and woman, marriage and family, society and civilization would be washed away.

Sword of Ishtar

If marriage was being weakened, so too was the family. Though the spirit of the times portrayed men and fathers as disposable, they were not. And their absence would have severe, long-term, and destructive repercussions on the next generation and on society as a whole. The example of husband and wife, father and mother in the lifelong covenant of marriage was becoming increasingly rare and alien to a new generation of children. The phenomenon had no precedent. American and Western society were entering uncharted territory.

It is easily forgotten that Ishtar was the goddess not only of sexuality—but destruction. She wielded a sword. The sword of Ishtar had now struck. And in the wake of its striking were the ruins of broken marriages, broken fathers, broken mothers, broken families, broken children, and broken lives, not to mention a broken generation, a broken culture, and a broken civilization.

◆◆◆

The goddess's work would go further and deeper still. Not only would she alter the purpose and nature of man and woman—she would erode the lines that separated them. She would merge them together.

Is it possible that what we are now witnessing in our culture concerning the merging of genders goes back to the goddess's ancient priesthood?

Chapter 30

The Androgynous

AVING USHERED IN the metamorphosis of gender, the goddess would now take it to the next stage and level.

The Assinnu, Kurgarru, Kalu, and Gala

It is one thing to demasculinize the one and defeminize the other, but it is another to superimpose the one onto the other or to merge the two.

But this was her power. It could be seen in her worship and priesthood. Her priests and ministers, her temple singers, and her ritual performers, the *assinnu*, the *kurgarru*, the *kalu*, and the *gala*, were known for publicly bending and breaking the parameters and definitions of gender. They were men who had taken on the appearances and attributes of women. As Ishtar had masculinized herself, her male priests had feminized themselves or had been feminized.

They made themselves to appear as women. They dressed in women's garments; they made up their faces. Today, they would be called cross-dressers, transvestites, nonbinary, bi-gender, or androgynous.

The Return of the Androgynous God

So the cult of Ishtar overflowed, not only with sexuality and promiscuity but androgyny. Ishtar herself, a female with male attributes, was an embodiment of androgyny. So too were her priests, as males with female attributes. One writer observed of the goddess:

> Her androgyny is attested to in her cultic personnel, which included eunuchs and transvestites and during her festival young men carried hoops, a feminine symbol, while young women carried swords.[1]

So what would happen if the spirit of Ishtar took possession of America and Western culture? We would expect to see the merging of male and female, the confusing of the two, the feminization of males and the masculinization of females. And this too is exactly what happened.

A strange thing accompanied the phenomenon. To speak of a man as being particularly masculine or manly or as especially possessing male traits was now increasingly looked upon with disdain. Similarly, to speak of a woman as being especially feminine, or wifely, fell into disfavor. If possessed by a male, maleness became a negative attribute. If possessed by a female, femininity became an attribute of little value and retrograde. On the other hand, if male traits were possessed by a woman, they were now to be celebrated and admired, and female traits, if possessed by a man, were now to be applauded as a virtue.

What could account for such a strange inversion of nature and reality? It was all in keeping with the spirit of the goddess who specialized in the masculinization of women and the feminization of men.

The Problem of Biology

Female icons of popular music and youth culture, unlike those of early generations, now reveled in appearing wild, unruly, shocking, vulgar, and aggressive. Many of their male counterparts, on the other hand, would adorn themselves with eyeliner and lipstick and other trappings of femininity or androgyny.

Cosmetics were now increasingly sold to male consumers. Attempts were made to masculinize women's fashion and feminize the fashion and appearance of men. This was precisely what the goddess would do—as attested by an ancient hymn sung in her praise:

> She ador[ns] a man as a woman, she ador[ns] a woman as a man.[2]

A concept that had never before existed in human history was invented to coincide with the metamorphosis. It was called *gender identity*. By this it was now possible to divorce oneself from one's biological being. Everyone was now told that they possessed a gender or sexual identity that could very well be the opposite of what they were born as, contrary to their biological gender.

All were now encouraged to consider whether they were, in fact, authentically other than what they were; men were to consider whether they were, in fact, women, and women, whether they were, in reality, men.

Kingdom of Magic

The young were especially vulnerable, as it was their elders and teachers telling them that this was, in fact, the truth. The seeds were planted for boys to wonder if they were actually girls, and girls, if they were boys.

Dresses, they were told, were for boys as well as girls. Girls could be princes, and boys could be princesses. Age-old fairy tales now had to be altered in order to ensure that princes no longer rescued the princesses and that the princesses now possessed a sufficient number of masculine attributes.

And if a boy or girl desired to see their favorite fairy-tale characters at Disney World®, he or she would find that "boys" and "girls" no longer existed.[3] The two words had now become a profanity never to be publicly spoken by the keepers of the Magic Kingdom®. They had been made to magically disappear. It was all magic—the magic of the goddess.

Ishtar's Storybook Hour

And if little children were not already sufficiently confused as to their sexual identities, they could now be brought to the public library, where a man wearing lipstick, false eyelashes, mascara, high heels, a wig, and a dress formed to simulate a woman's anatomy would read to them their favorite children's storybooks. They had once ministered as priests in the temples of Ishtar. Now they ministered to children in public libraries.

In an ancient Hittite prayer, Ishtar is described as possessing the power to

> ...make young women dress as men on their right side, to
> make young men dress as women on their left side.[4]

So the spirit of Ishtar now again made young women dress as men and young men dress as women and both dress as both—and as neither. A strange spirit was now leading the culture in which adults now seemed to take great delight in encouraging children to take on the dress and attributes of the opposite gender.

Return of the Gala Priest

After ages of absence from the mainstream of Western civilization, transvestites, or, as they were now often called, drag queens, began emerging from the shadows and onto the center stage of mainstream culture.

In the days of the goddess they had basked in the limelight of ancient pagan temples as her gala priests. She had returned. So it was inevitable that they would return as well. As in their ancient glory days, they were now again celebrated and enshrined in the limelight of mainstream culture.

They had returned with the goddess to again officiate, minister, and preside as high priests of modern culture.

————◆◆◆————

And still the goddess was not finished. There was another step, another realm to be entered, and another transformation to be set in motion.

This one would most converge on a specific site, at a specific time—a specific event.

It would be there, in the streets of New York City, that the goddess would take her stand and from there that she would cast a new spell and set in motion a new metamorphosis that would change American culture and that of the world.

Chapter 31

Priests, Gods, and Shadows

IT WAS THE line that the goddess crossed at the end of the 1960s that would trigger a metamorphosis of morality, ethics, values, society, culture, perception, and human nature of seismic proportions.

The Altering of Desire

It was all there, implicit from the beginning, and made clear, over and over again, in the ancient inscriptions:

> May Ishtar, Mistress of battle and conflict, turn his masculinity into femininity.[1]

She was continually praised for her power to *"turn a man into a woman and a woman into a man."*[2] Implicit in the changing of sexuality is the changing of desire. A man transformed by the goddess into a woman would presumably now desire men. A woman changed into a man would presumably desire women. This brings us into the realm of altered desire.

The goddess herself boasted of being able to change back and forth between female and male. Though unspoken, it would be implicit that her desire as a woman would be for a man and as a man, for a woman. Beyond that she was the one especially invoked when one was seeking to alter another's romantic or sexual desire. She was the sorceress. It was her power to change desire.

Then there were her priests, her performers, the cultic ministers of her temples, the men who dressed in female garments and took on female appearance. They would serve as examples of her power to alter sexuality. But their transformation went beyond clothing or outward appearance. Some took on women's names. Some would sing the cultic songs in the female dialect. Some even took on roles akin to consorts or wives.

Exile of the Assinnu

Thus it was more than appearance or mannerisms. It was sexual. Ancient Akkadian texts give instructions to men on having sexual relations with the assinnu, Ishtar's feminized men. It was thus a feature of the goddess's worship for her male priests to perform sexual acts with other men. A large part of Ishtar's priesthood would today be classified as *homosexuals* or *gay*, and her cult as one of androgyny, transvestitism, and cross-genderism.

When Western civilization turned away from paganism and the gods and goddesses went into exile, the condoning of homosexuality and other related behaviors came to an end. When the goddess went into exile and her temples closed, the assinnu priests and her other cross-gendered cultic personnel left the temples and followed the goddess into exile. They disappeared.

In the new era and civilization, gender-crossing practices such as homosexuality and transvestitism would be seen as immoral, sinful, inversions of the natural order. Such things would now be proscribed by codes of morality, societal convention, law, and Scripture. The licentiousness and transgressions for which the goddess's sanctuaries were known would now fade into history, become distant memories, and then be forgotten.

The Emergence of the Shadow Men

But if the goddess was to return, what would we expect to happen? We would expect that the values and practices of her cult and worship would return as well.

In other words, if the goddess whose religion involved the acceptance, the open practice, the sanctification, and the enshrinement of homosexuality was to return, then her return would again bring about the acceptance, the open practice, and the sanctification of homosexuality, and its re-enshrinement in Western civilization. And that is exactly what would happen.

The goddess would cause homosexuality to come out of the shadows, out of the realm of the forbidden, and introduce it to a civilization to which it was alien and taboo. And when that would take place, it would not be so much a diverting of the sexual revolution but its logical conclusion.

The Two Priesthoods

The dynamic could be seen in the goddess's ancient cult of worship. Her female priests and workers, the *harimtu*, the *kezertu*, the *samhatu*, and the *istaru*, engaged in sexual activity outside of marriage, but they did so with men. So sexuality was at first removed from the one context, that of the marital covenant, but remained within the other, male-female sexuality.

But with Ishtar's male priesthood, from the assinnu to the gala, the divorcing of sexuality from its natural or traditional context, its decontextualization, was taken to another level. The goddess's male priests removed sexuality from gender, from its biological context of male and female. Thus they represented a deeper level of decontextualization. One priesthood led into the other—or one stage of decontextualization and deconstruction would lead into the next.

The Deconstruction of Sex

In the same way, it was the sexual revolution that led to the normalization of homosexuality. If sexuality could be removed from the context of marriage, as in the sexual revolution, then it could also be removed from the context of gender, as in the normalization of homosexuality.

It was for that reason that the seminal event that introduced homosexuality into the mainstream of Western civilization did not take place at the beginning of the sexual revolution in the early 1960s but at the decade's end. And as with Ishtar's male priesthood, it would represent a further and deeper stage in the decontextualization and deconstruction of sexuality.

It went hand in hand with another of the goddess's works. She had already begun separating husbands and wives and blurring the distinctions between male and female. If men and women were now interchangeable in every other realm, then it was only a matter of time before they would be seen as interchangeable in the realm of sexuality. So the emergence of homosexuality in American and Western culture was the fruit of several movements, all of which had a common denominator—the goddess.

Seismic Night

It would all come to a head in 1969, on a summer night on the streets of New York City—in an explosion. It concerned a bar called the Stonewall Inn. It would lead into days of rage and violence and would trigger a new movement and a cultural transformation.

It was there in the streets of New York City that the goddess would make her stand and bring what had been hidden in the shadows into the spotlight of American culture, then Western culture, and finally the world.

Her agenda was ultimately to take a Christian civilization, alter its values, its perception of marriage, gender, and sexuality, until it had been transformed into a pagan civilization. As with the other transformations, it would have to be carried out step by step, first by mentioning the unmentionable, then by making the shocking familiar. From there the culture would be moved to toleration, then acceptance. That which was once unmentionable would become established, celebrated, championed, and then enforced.

As she had introduced the transformation on the streets of New York, she would then introduce it into media, film, theater, television, music, politics, law, the educational system, children's cartoons, cereal boxes, everywhere. It would continue its saturation until there was hardly a facet of modern culture that had not been touched or altered by it. Laws would be overturned, and what was formerly illegal would now be celebrated.

The overturning of something so basic to civilization as the male-female paradigm and norm would prove especially potent in the transformation of American and Western culture.

The Other Coming Out

When the gods departed from Western civilization, the open practice of homosexuality went with them. Both disappeared into the shadows and fringes. Therefore, the reappearance of homosexuality onto the center stage of Western civilization, its reemergence from the shadows and closets of that civilization after two thousand years, was a sign—there were others who were also reemerging. There were likewise coming out of the shadows at the fringes of Western civilization after two thousand years—the gods.

Round 2

It would signify, as well, another change of colossal magnitude. With the disappearance of the gods and that of the open practice of homosexuality, it was a sign that Western civilization had turned to the gospel, to the Christian faith. Therefore, the return of homosexuality to the center of Western civilization was a sign not only of the return of gods but of a seismic change with regard to spirituality. It was a sign that Western civilization was turning away from the Christian faith. After nearly two thousand years the bond joining together that civilization and that faith was beginning to dissolve.

Each major step taken toward the establishment of homosexuality would be matched by an inverse step toward the disestablishment of Christianity. Every movement to celebrate homosexuality would lead to an inverse movement away from Judeo-Christian faith or the attacking of biblical values. The embracing of the morality embodied by the goddess was both a measure of and an instrument for the dechristianization of America and Western civilization.

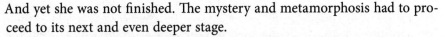

The goddess was now casting a deeper spell. She had altered desires and the perception of a nation. The civilization that had once stood for Christian values was now championing the very things it had once condemned and condemning the very things it had once championed. It was celebrating what it had once forbidden and forbidding what it had once celebrated. America and Western culture would be converted and would become pagan.

And yet she was not finished. The mystery and metamorphosis had to proceed to its next and even deeper stage.

What would happen next had its origins in the goddess's ancient hymns, in the ministers of her cult, in her powers, and in a mysterious entity from her mythology.

Chapter 32

The Altered

THE NEXT STAGE in the transforming of sexuality and gender would strike many as especially strange and alien, and yet its origins were ancient, and its mystery could be found in the temples of the goddess.

The Work of a Sorceress

That the power of the goddess was "to turn a man into a woman and a woman into a man, to change one into the other"[1] implies more than the clothing of transvestitism, the desires of homosexuality, or even an identification with the opposite sex. In its most literal or ultimate understanding, it would mean the actual transformation of a man into a woman and a woman into a man. It would mean that the goddess had the power to physically transform a member of one sex into the other.

It was, again, the act of magic, the work of a sorceress. To turn a man into a woman and a woman into a man was to transition one sex into another. It was an act of transsexualization or transgenderism. The person so transitioned by the goddess had become transsexual.

Ninshubar

Ishtar's personal assistant was a deity named Ninshubar. Ninshubar was female, a goddess. But she was of a strange nature. She continually changed her genders. In the service of other gods Ninshubar was male. But in the presence of Ishtar she became female—and back and forth again. Thus Ishtar's assistant was a transsexual being.

It was Ishtar who would transform herself from female to male and back again. In this sense Ishtar herself was transsexual. So it should be no surprise that transsexuality should appear in both her mythology and her worship.

The Intersex Beings

In the myth of her descent to the underworld and her imprisonment there, two beings were created to enable her escape. One was called the *kurgarra*, and the other, the *galatur*. They were described as intersex beings, not quite one or the other, or those who moved in between the two. The names *kurgarra* and *galatur* were also the titles of the gender-crossing cultic personnel that ministered in Ishtar's temples.

In the Akkadian version of the myth, the being sent to rescue Ishtar from the underworld was called Asushunamir, the *assinnu*. Again, it was an intersexual, transsexual, or transgender entity, and again, the name, or appellation, was also the title of Ishtar's cultic ministers, the *assinnu*. In fact, the meaning of the name *assinnu* is *"man-woman."*

An ancient description of the goddess's ministers says this:

> They turned out the [kurgarrû] and [assinnu] (at) Eanna,
> *whose manhood Ishtar changed to womanhood* to strike
> awe into the people.[2]

The Surgeon Goddess

To transform manhood into womanhood to *"strike awe into the people"* would speak of something more substantial than effeminate behaviors and the wearing of women's garments. An ancient inscription from southern Turkey speaks of Ishtar's altering of sexuality in especially graphic terms:

> May Ishtar…impress feminine parts into his male parts.[3]

The cult of the goddess is believed to have involved castration. Many of her priests and cultic personnel are believed to have been eunuchs, having been castrated as part of obtaining the position or having been castrated earlier in their lives. Some are believed to have castrated themselves. Later historical accounts describe the worshippers and cultic personnel of related deities as castrating themselves in the midst of worship. In one way or another, they were surgically altered.

It was, for them, an attempt to rid themselves of the characteristics of the gender in which they were born and move one step closer to the gender they sought to emulate. Because of their castration the amount of the male hormone testosterone that circulated in their bodies would be drastically reduced. This, in turn, would lead to the minimizing of other male characteristics. All this was combined with the wearing of women's garments and adornments. The goddess's priests and cultic ministers were the transsexuals of the ancient world.

A More Extreme Stage

So if the goddess was to return to the modern world, what would we expect to take place? We would expect the trappings and characteristics of her priesthood to likewise return. We would expect her powers to transform sexuality and gender to again be demonstrated. In short, we would expect the return of transsexuality or transgenderism. And this, again, is exactly what happened.

Transsexuality and transgenderism represent a more extreme form or stage in the blurring and deconstruction of gender than that of transvestitism and homosexuality. Therefore, we would expect the return of transsexuality and transgenderism to mainstream culture to happen at a still later stage in the goddess's transformations. And so it did.

The very first attempts at surgically altering an individual's sexuality were made in the early twentieth century. By the 1960s the procedure was still an extremely rare oddity. The terms *transgenderism* and *transgenderal* first appeared in the mid- to late 1960s. The term *transgender* is believed to have been officially coined in 1965. It was in the 1990s that the term first attained widespread usage.

But it was in the twenty-first century that the phenomenon of transsexuality or transgenderism exploded onto the stage of world culture, centering, again, on the focal point of the goddess's return, America and Western culture.

The Vulnerable

Ishtar was most often portrayed as a young woman. When she spoke of her transitioning from one gender to another, she spoke of becoming an *"exuberant young man"* or a *"noble young man."*[4]

The word *young* is of significance. If the gods are to alter a nation or transform a civilization, if they are to take control of its future, they must, as we have seen, possess its young. And so when it came to the confusing of gender and the breaking of its distinctions, it was the young who would be especially vulnerable.

No generation had been so subjected to a barrage of gender blurring and confusion as that which came of age in the early part of the twenty-first century. And it was then that a massive change took place. The number of young people and children in America and the West identifying as transgender in America exploded. From 2009 to 2018 the number of girls seeking gender transition treatments in the United Kingdom alone skyrocketed by

4,515 percent.[5] It was another phenomenon unprecedented in human history.

What was equally unprecedented was the fact that the greatest increases in those seeking or being referred to "gender reassignment" were now young women. A generation possessed by the goddess was now doing as the goddess boasted of having done. *Young women* were now seeking to become *young men*.

Suffer the Little Children

The altering of children's bodies now became big business. Abortion facilities all over America added the transitioning of males into females and females into males to their services of killing unborn children. In this they performed, under one roof, the rites of multiple gods.

And since children were a captive audience as they sat in their classrooms, the spirit of the goddess came upon the public school system. Schoolchildren were now being inducted into transgenderism through the words and authority of their teachers. They would be taught that they could decide if they were to be a boy or girl. They would then be questioned as to what sex they really were and if they were not actually other than they had thought they were. They would then be led into the process of being transitioned. They were too young to understand the ramifications of what was happening. The process of "*reassigning*" their gender would begin, often while their parents were kept from knowing what was happening to their child.

The Altered

Children's entertainment, cartoons, video games, television, social media, movies, and other children's media and influences joined in the barrage. As a result, masses of children were subjected to hormonal treatments that would irreversibly alter and damage their bodies, their health, and their lives. Many of them were transitioned and sterilized for life before they even knew what sexuality was.

Celebrities, government leaders, educators, business leaders, physicians, surgeons, and activists all joined the crusade to promote the altering of children. It defied rationality and common sense. What could have possessed them to embrace and champion such a thing that, in any previous generation, would have been viewed as madness?

What possessed them was the spirit of the goddess. And so multitudes of children and youths were now being inducted into the metamorphosis undergone by the priests and ministers of the goddess in order to become her servants.

But unlike in ancient times, the goddess was not interested in merely one class of people to serve as her priesthood—she was now after an entire generation. And an entire generation was now being prepared to embody, in one form or another, the gender confusion of the goddess and to unwittingly serve as her priesthood.

And it was not the goddess alone. The gods had always had a special interest in destroying children. If their sacrificial knives could not touch them before their births, they would touch them now.

An Idol of One's Own Being

If, in a pagan universe, one fashions one's own idol, builds one's own god, and thus creates one's own reality, then in such a universe, one can create or re-create the reality of oneself. So as the work of the gods and the paganization of the West progressed, a woman could decide that her personal reality was that she was actually a man or, for that matter, an animal or any other being.

But in order to put one's reality into effect, one must nullify the reality that actually exists. Thus in order to create what is *not* reality, one must nullify what *is* reality. And to re-create oneself, one must nullify one's own existence. Self-creation thus becomes an act of self-destruction.

And to create one's own reality is to make an idol. And to create it out of oneself is to make an idol of one's own being. And in the act of transitioning, one must carve the idol so that it conforms to the reality one wants to create. And so the alteration of gender would always involve the act of self-destruction.

The Destruction of Women

The destruction would go beyond that of individuals. It would affect society as a whole. Feminists began noticing a new phenomenon: the destruction or erasure of women. The word *women* was being struck from official documents and discourse—replaced with phrases such as "people with uteruses" or not replaced at all. Men too were being erased. So too were sisters and brothers, mothers and fathers, sons and daughters, boys and girls, ladies and gentlemen.

The Abolition of Man

It was the mission of the gods to eradicate human nature, humanity—the abolition of man. They promised that one could do with one's being and life whatever one believed or imagined. But if one could give one's life and being to *any* purpose, it would mean that one's life and being had *no* real, intrinsic, absolute, or ultimate purpose. And if there is no absolute or ultimate purpose to one's life, then one's life has no ultimate meaning or value.

And thus one's life becomes disposable—man, woman, humanity, each person, each life. Thus what the gods presented as freedom was, actually, destruction, and what they promised as fulfillment was, in the end, the abolition of man.

—————◆◆◆—————

Is it possible that one of the most pivotal movements of modern times was not only begun by the goddess but indwelled at its birth by her presence?

Is it possible that the event that triggered this movement not only was saturated with the elements of her mythology—but was its replaying?

We are now about to remove the veil on an event that altered American and world culture. In its removal we will see how an ancient Mesopotamian deity indwelled the streets of New York City.

Part VIII:

EXPLOSION

Chapter 33

Night of the Goddess

T HE RETURN OF the goddess could be discerned from the beginning of the sexual revolution. But what we are about to see is how a single event would embody her entrance into modern culture in a way no other event ever had. More than any other, this one event would open the door for the altering of values in the realm of sexuality, marriage, gender, family, even the Bible, Christianity, and the ways of God.

Stonewall

It would be known as *Stonewall*. It would come to be commemorated every year in nearly every part of the globe. It would represent an explosion that would begin a leavening through American culture, Western culture, and then the world.

Is it possible that this event was not only a conflagration of social unrest, disorder, and upheaval but of spiritual forces? Is it possible that behind it all was the spirit of the goddess—*and her mythology*?

What is now known as *Stonewall*, or the *Stonewall riots*, or the *Stonewall uprising*, took its name from the Stonewall Inn, a gay bar of Greenwich Village in New York City. As with other gay bars in the city, it was owned and operated by the Mafia. In late June of 1969 the police raided it. Such raids were not uncommon for several reasons. Beyond the fact that homosexual acts were not legal, the bar was operating illegally without a proper liquor license. The bar owners would typically bribe the police to allow them to function, and the police, on their part, would often alert the owners before carrying out a raid.

Explosion

The raid began in the early hours of the night. There were an estimated two hundred people at the bar that night. During the raid the police cleared most of them out and focused their efforts on the bar's employees and a number of cross-dressers whom they pressed for identification. Soon they began loading some of those they had kept for questioning into a police van.

The multitude of patrons remained standing outside, along with curious onlookers. During one of the arrests something took hold of the crowd, an agitation, then a spirit of rage, and then an explosion. The crowd started taunting the police officers and then hurling objects at them—bottles, rocks, and, reportedly, bricks. The rage was so fierce and the situation so dangerous that the police retreated into the bar, barricading themselves in fear of their lives. The crowd then came after them, charging the bar, attempting to break open its front door to get to them.

Eventually help came for the barricaded police, but the rage and uprising went on. The "Stonewall riots" continued for days. At the time, it appeared as an oddity, a disturbance on the fringes of society. Most people had no idea it had even happened. But the repercussions of what happened that night would grow and deepen with the passing of each year. In time, those joining the commemorations of Stonewall and the movement it represented would number in the multiplied millions.

Ancient Doors and Spirits

We have spoken of the door that had closed to the gods in ancient times. Stonewall was a key part of its reopening. In view of that it should come as no surprise that it was an event of rage, upheaval, and violence. The ancient door was now being pummeled and forced to open. Spirits were entering in, and gods were returning.

And so with regard to the realm of spirits and gods, what took place at Stonewall was of great significance. And it was not only the police and the multitudes who were there that night. But in the midst of the crowd was the goddess.

What happened that night went beyond the natural realm. Those involved in it, no matter what side they were on, had no idea. They were only vessels, or pawns, in an ancient mystery.

We are now going to pull back the veil on what took place on that June night in New York City. Behind that veil we will discover another realm, a world of convergences, spirits and flesh, the ancient world and the modern, the mythological and the real.

◆◆◆

Was there a reason that what happened that night had to take place in New York City?

And is it possible that the reason goes back to the goddess and her mythology?

Chapter 34

The Wondrous Gate

THE RETURN OF the goddess had ushered in the sexual revolution, but the revolution that was now about to begin would require its own entrance. The goddess would need a portal through which to enter and by which to bring back into Western civilization that which had been kept out. She would need to come to the gate.

Ishtar at the Gate

Ishtar had always been drawn to gates. Among her most prominent symbols was a pair of standards referred to as gateposts. And one of the most famous of all archaeological remains is that of the Ishtar Gate that opened the way to the city of Babylon.

So too gates played a central role in her descent to the underworld. She demanded their opening. She would open them one way or another. It was her nature; she was the trespasser of boundaries.

What she was now about to force open was the long-closed door, the locked gateway of Western civilization. She would have to come to the gateway to do it. In the late twentieth century America was the leading power of Western civilization and of what could still be called Christian civilization. She would come to its gateway.

The Goddess in New York City

America had one gateway above all others. It was the gateway through which millions entered and departed the nation, and through which trade, commerce, commodities, culture, and ideas poured in and out. It was the gate by which its most iconic statue lifted up its lamp "beside the golden door."[1] The gate was, of course, New York City. So the goddess who, in ancient times, was always drawn to the gate would now, upon her return, come to the central gate of American and Western civilization, New York City.

An Offering of Firstfruits

One of the ancient inscriptions of her mythology tells of how she approached a "wondrous gate":

> In the evening, she came forth with authority and stood in the street before a wondrous gate. She made an offering of firstfruits.[2]

So now again, the goddess would come "in the evening" and stand "in the street" before America's "wondrous gate," New York City. In the myth she makes an offering of "firstfruits." *Firstfruits* refers to an offering or sacrifice that marks a beginning. So the goddess would now lift up her offering at the gate of America, the firstfruits, the beginning of a movement that would transform American culture and the world.

So there, at America's gateway, she would begin the opening of the ancient door. It would not open freely. But she was the goddess who boasted of the power to force open what had been closed to her.

Open Your Gate

In the mythology of her descent to the underworld, she stands at the gate and calls out:

> Gate-keeper, ho, open your gate! Open your gate that I may enter![3]

She would not be kept out. So in the summer of 1969, the goddess came to the gate and to Stonewall. That night, her spirit would indwell the multitude, who would then demand that long-closed door be opened to them. That night, it would all begin. And the movement that would transform world culture would begin, as it had to, at the gate.

What is the eshdam?

And could it have pinpointed the exact location in which the explosion had to take place?

Chapter 35

The Eshdam

ISHTAR DWELLED IN a place called the *eshdam*. What was it?

The Tavern

Eshdam was the ancient Mesopotamian word for a tavern, pub, or inn. The tavern was especially linked to the goddess. She was the protector of the eshdam, the patroness of taverns. Of the goddess's special relationship to the tavern, one writer observed:

> From this period and into the first millennium BCE, the tavern or alehouse was Inanna/Ishtar's special province and one that she personally safeguarded.[1]

The ancient hymns that sing her praise make a point of noting the connection between the two. The goddess sits in the eshdam and there makes her living. The connection between the two was so strong that the eshdam could be seen as her home. One writer notes,

> It may be that images of "her home," as the tavern was sometimes called, automatically enlisted that aspect of Inanna [*Ishtar*] which specifically protected the local pub.[2]

The Stonewall Eshdam

The goddess not only dwelled in the tavern but would use it for her purposes. So upon her return to the modern world, it was not only that she would enter by the gate, but that she would be sure to find an eshdam, a tavern, to use for her purposes. And so it was no accident that on that evening in the last days of June 1969, the workings of the goddess would converge as they had in ancient times—on an eshdam. In this case, the eshdam was called Stonewall.

Stonewall was the fulfillment of the ancient Mesopotamian word. It was a tavern, a bar, an alehouse. It was the natural setting for the goddess's dwelling and workings. There was hardly another place on earth more fitting by which to make her entrance. It had to begin there.

House of Ale

Ishtar's ancient eshdams were known for one alcoholic beverage in particular—beer. The word can more specifically also be translated as *beer house* or *alehouse*. The goddess dwelled in a house of beer.

So Stonewall was especially known for one beverage above all others—beer. Visitors described it as being heavily saturated with the smell of beer. So as soon as one walked through its doors, one was met with the aroma of the eshdam.

Beer was also central in the sacred libations offered up to Ishtar and the gods. Fermenting vats were used in religious rituals, spells, and incantations. The liquid was believed to possess magical powers. The eshdam or alehouse was believed to be a supernaturally charged space in possession of the goddess. So on that hot summer night of 1969, the eshdam would again become supernaturally charged and possessed by the goddess.

House of Altered Gender

Another element of the eshdam was sexuality. The goddess confessed to using the eshdam to procure sexual relationships. So at Stonewall the element of sexuality was ever present. It was the issue of sexuality that distinguished Stonewall from most other bars in the city. And it was that issue of sexuality that ignited the explosion.

The goddess connects her altering of gender to a particular place:

> When I sit in *the alehouse* [*eshdam*], I am a woman, and I am
> an exuberant young man.[3]

Thus in the presence of the goddess, the eshdam became the place where the lines of gender were blurred and broken and where the nature of sexuality was altered, where a woman became a man and a man, a woman.

And so it was with Stonewall; it was the eshdam where the lines of gender were blurred, crossed, and broken. It was the eshdam in which sexuality was altered and from which that altering would spread to the world.

Judgment House

The eshdam would play another role in Ishtar's mythology:

> The holy Inanna [*Ishtar*] made enter [*her*] eshdam,
> She stood in judgment, decreed [*their*] fate.[4]

The goddess is described as entering the eshdam or alehouse to bring vengeance. The eshdam thus becomes the goddess's ground on which to redress her grievances, punish offenses, and exact retribution. On the night the riot began, the eshdam of Stonewall again became the site where offenses were punished, grievances redressed, and scores evened.

That night, the multitude, inflamed by the spirit of the goddess, attempted to *enter her eshdam* and stand in judgment against a civilization they believed had sinned against them.

Go Down to Your Alehouse

One Mesopotamian text says this of the goddess:

Harlot, you go down to the alehouse.[5]

So in the summer of 1969, the goddess known as "the harlot" went "down to the alehouse"—Ishtar went down to Stonewall.

Though it might come across as strange to Western ears, in ancient Mesopotamian texts the word for *tavern* or *alehouse* is, at times, joined to the Mesopotamian word for *holy*. The goddess is spoken of as possessing the "*holy eshdam,*" the "*sacred alehouse,*" the "*holy tavern.*"[6] The tavern became something akin to her temple, hallowed ground. And so the bar known as Stonewall would become enshrined as a holy place. It was no accident that the movement that disseminated the ways of the goddess would hallow as its sacred shrine its temple, Stonewall, its "*sacred alehouse,*" the "*holy eshdam.*"

◆◆◆

There was more to the goddess's dwelling place, or eshdam. One more element from her mythology was needed to complete it.

It would be there at Stonewall. And it would play a central part in the explosion of that night.

Chapter 36

House of the Harimtu

ISHTAR WAS GODDESS and patroness of taverns and prostitutes. We would therefore expect the two to come together.

The Alehouse Harlot

In one of the Mesopotamian myths that speak of her powers and possessions, the goddess is told

> ...you have brought with you the cultic prostitute, you have brought with you the holy tavern.[1]

She was in charge of the prostitute and the "*holy tavern*." As goddess of the *harimtu*, or prostitute, and of the *eshdam*, or alehouse, Ishtar was the embodiment of both. She was the *eshdam harimtu*, the alehouse harlot, or tavern prostitute. In one of her hymns the goddess says this:

> *When I sit by the gate of the tavern*, I am a prostitute.[2]

Here, the three elements of the goddess converge: the gate; the tavern, or alehouse; and the prostitute. The tavern, if not an official house of prostitution, was a house in which prostitutes dwelled and operated.

The Stonewall Prostitutes

So could the other element of the goddess, that of the prostitute, also have manifested on the night of Stonewall?

It did. Talk and rumors of prostitution had always surrounded the bar. There were reports of a prostitution ring being operated on the second floor. There were even reports of prostitution taking place within the bar itself.

But beyond that was Stonewall's other and more visible link to prostitution. The tavern had become a center, a haven and gathering place, for the male prostitutes, sex workers, and street hustlers of lower Manhattan. The prostitution over which Ishtar presided in ancient times was not confined to female sex workers. The functions of the assinnu, Ishtar's feminized males, undoubtedly overlapped into the realm and functions of prostitution. A Sumerian inscription describing the goddess's festivals says this:

Tightening their hairgrips for her, male prostitutes parade before her, holy Inana [Ishtar]. Their locks of hair at the back are adorned for her with coloured rags.[3]

The Harimtu Revolution

Not only were male prostitutes a central part of the Stonewall Inn, but they actually *led the uprising.* One of the most prominent leaders in that uprising and in the movement that followed was a drag performer named Marsha Johnson, who worked at night as a male prostitute. She was one among several others.

So on that summer night at Stonewall, the two elements, the harimtu and the eshdam, the prostitute and the alehouse, converged just as they had converged in ancient times under the patronage of the goddess.

That night, the goddess's modern-day assinnu, her male prostitutes, were there on the streets, gathered around her modern-day eshdam, to ignite the explosion.

So the movement that would transform Western culture was started by prostitutes, just as it was begun by the prostitute goddess—the alehouse harlot.

◆◆◆

But why Stonewall? Why there as opposed to other taverns or alehouses?

Was there something more to it?

Is it possible that the answer lies in ancient tablets that pinpointed Stonewall as the place in which it had to happen?

Chapter 37

The Stonewall

THE GODDESS HAD always been known as the one who broke down barriers. She came to New York for that purpose. So there could not have been a more appropriate name for the place where she would break down that barrier than *Stonewall*.

But could there be more to the mystery?

The Goddess on the Wall

The *Epic of Gilgamesh* contains a vivid description of the goddess's rage. Ishtar attempts to seduce the hero Gilgamesh. Gilgamesh, in a blunt and cutting discourse, spurns her advances. Ishtar retaliates by calling down the "*bull of heaven*" to wreak destruction on the earth. Gilgamesh and his associate, Enkidu, slay the bull. Ishtar then

...mounted the great wall of Uruk.[1]

The goddess takes her stand on top of the city wall and there gives vent to her anguish and anger and calls down curses on those who offended her. So the goddess who vented her fury on the city wall now, on the night that she would vent her fury on an entire civilization, chose as her focal point the place called Stonewall. There she took her stand and made it her platform. And from there she unleashed her anguish and fury.

The Wall of Uruk

The ancient wall of Uruk on which the goddess stood was made up of bricks. On the night of Stonewall, bricks had a prominent place. The Stonewall Inn itself was known for its facade, a wall of bricks.

Beyond that the Stonewall riots were begun with the hurling of objects at the police. No one knows exactly what those first objects were, but it was reported to have been bricks. Bricks became a key part of the Stonewall mythology. The question "Who threw the first brick at Stonewall?" became a rallying cry for the movement. It is known that brick-like stones were dug up from nearby tree pits and were among the objects hurled at the police officers at the beginning of the uprising.

The Stone and the Stonewall

The immediate event that led Ishtar to stand on the wall and cast down her curses was Gilgamesh's slaying of the bull of heaven. But behind the slaying, the seminal offense that triggered all that followed was Gilgamesh's scathing rejection of the goddess's advances. As she stands on the wall, it is the first thing she speaks of:

> Woe unto Gilgamesh who slandered me.[2]

How had Gilgamesh slandered the goddess? He presented a case against her. If he became her lover, it would bring him calamity and sorrow as it had her past lovers, Tammuz and a long line of others. The goddess brought harm and destruction to those who loved her. She was toxic, unstable, and deadly.

In his devastating attack on her history and nature, he used pictures, symbols. One of these is of particular note. The goddess, he said, is a stone

> …that buckles out the *stone wall*.[3]

The Other Stone Wall

Thousands of years before the uprising of Stonewall, the words *"stone wall"* were inscribed on clay tablets. The word *stonewall* was used in connection with the goddess of sexuality, of taverns, of prostitutes, of transvestitism, transsexuality, homosexuality, and the crossing of genders.

"Stone wall" were the words and symbol used to speak of the goddess's destructive consequences on the world around her and specifically on her own people, her lovers. *Stonewall* was used in the condemnation that caused her offense and ignited her fury.

Now the word *Stonewall* would again be joined to the goddess. Again, it would be used to cause her offense and ignite her fury. And again, it would become the symbol of her rage. The riots that erupted that night would leave Stonewall broken, burnt, and shattered. According to the ancient accusation in the *Epic of Gilgamesh*, the goddess would cause the "stone wall" to buckle.

It was the most fitting of names and places. For at Stonewall the goddess would cause another wall, a wall of ancient origins—the moral hedge that had served Western civilization for nearly two thousand years—to likewise buckle and collapse.

◆◆◆

There was an ancient symbol linked to the goddess's power. It would accompany her when she entered into battle. It was the first sign of her coming.

Therefore, when the goddess entered into battle at Stonewall, is it possible that she was accompanied by her ancient sign and that it was the first sign of her coming there?

Chapter 38

The Lion's Head

WITH THE EXCEPTION of the planet Venus, the Star of Ishtar, no other image was so prominently associated with the goddess as was the lion.

Labbatu—the Lioness

The goddess was called *Labbatu*, the *Lioness*. The title spoke of her power, her ferocity, and her savagery in battle. It appears in several ancient prayers and poems:

Inanna [*Ishtar*], great light, lioness of heaven...[1]

My lady, lioness of battles, who challenges foreign lands...[2]

In heaven and on earth you roar like a lion and devastate the people....Like a fearsome lion you pacify the insubordinate and unsubmissive with your gall.[3]

...on harnessed lions, she cuts to pieces him who shows no respect.[4]

She Who Rides the Lion

No other animal was so associated with the goddess. None other so graphically embodied her. It was the "symbol of her divinity."[5] It was the lion that carried her into battle.

She is described as riding a chariot driven by seven lions. And in carved reliefs, she stands on the back of a lion or lions as she rides into war. Her power was so great that even the king of beasts yielded to her will and obeyed her commands. Thus the lion was her chosen platform from which she would wage war and inflict vengeance.

The Lion's Head

But there was one part of the animal that most strongly displayed her power and dominance—the lion's head. The goddess is depicted in carved reliefs as holding reins, by which she turns the lion's head and directs the course of her entrance. In other reliefs she places her foot on top of the lion's head. It was a sign of total dominance and uncontested power. Ishtar was the goddess who stood on the lion's head. Then there was the tactical dimension—the lion's head was the first, most glaring, and most terrifying sight that an enemy would see as Ishtar approached to wreak destruction.

The lion's head became, in and of itself, a symbol of her power. It was the lion's head that crowned her scepter. And when she rode into battle, she would often brandish a curved sword, a scimitar, crowned with the lion's head. The symbol would serve as a reminder to her adversaries of the ferocity of her destructive power.

The Other Eshdam

If the goddess was to enter into battle, to engage in spiritual and cultural warfare, is it possible that the sign that accompanied her entrance into warfare in ancient times would manifest again? If Stonewall and Greenwich Village were to be the site where the war was to be launched, is it possible that the sign of her approach would specifically manifest there?

The sign appeared. And it did so in the same setting as did Stonewall—in fact, on the same street. It appeared just two doors down from Stonewall's front entrance. Like Stonewall, it was a bar, an alehouse, an eshdam, dwelling place of the goddess. It chose as its symbol and its name a part of an animal. It was called the *Lion's Head*—the same sign that, in ancient times, represented the power of the goddess as she entered into war.

The Sign of Her Approaching

As the lion's head would be the first sight of the goddess's approach in battle, so the Lion's Head tavern appeared in Greenwich Village in 1966. It was the first sign of what was approaching. Later that same year three members of the Mafia purchased the property that would become Stonewall. The following year, 1967, Stonewall opened its door. So as in ancient times, the lion's head was the first sign that the goddess was coming.

In ancient times the lion's head had accompanied the goddess into war. It would again. Its appearance on Christopher Street in Greenwich Village was the first sign that a war was about to begin and that it would be led by the goddess.

Standing on the Lion's Head

After the Stonewall uprising, one of the leading organizations of gay advocacy set up offices in Greenwich Village. Its headquarters were now located directly above the Lion's Head. It would now wage the goddess's war just as the goddess had waged her wars in ancient times, stationed on top of the symbol of her power—the lion's head.

◆◆◆

To the goddess was the power to seize and possess human vessels.

If she was the principality behind the uprising at Stonewall, if she was inciting it, then is it possible that on the night of the uprising she exercised the power to seize and possess?

Is it possible that those who played a key part in igniting the explosion were acting as her avatars?

And is it possible that one of them even appeared in her image?

Chapter 39

The Avatars

THE WORD *AVATAR* comes from a Sanskrit root word meaning descent. In Eastern religion it speaks of the descent or manifestation of a deity in bodily form, an incarnation. We will use it here to speak of a human being who serves as a vessel for the incarnation of a god, as in a spirit—a host.

Ishtar's Avatars

The phenomenon, as we have seen, was common in ancient times and in pagan cultures where the spirit of a god possessed its worshippers. We saw it in the ancient priests and priestesses who served as messengers of the gods. And we saw that the goddess Ishtar was especially known for possessing human vessels.

So could the goddess, upon her return, use and inhabit a human vessel? Could her spirit possess and animate that vessel to act as her proxy? Could there have been at Stonewall an avatar?

The Warrior Woman

If so, we would expect her to be, like the goddess, female. And yet it would seem unlikely for a woman to play a central role in the Stonewall uprising, as the overwhelming majority—some would say as much as 98 percent—of the bar's patrons were male. But there was at Stonewall that night a human vessel, a host, an avatar of the goddess. And it was a woman.

We might expect the avatar to have been, like the goddess, female but with male attributes. And this is exactly what she was—a woman with male attributes. As Ishtar was a fighter, we might expect her avatar to be as well.

And so she was. As Ishtar was fierce, so too was her avatar. And it was this one in the likeness of the goddess who would serve as the primary instrument to ignite the uprising.

Arresting the Goddess

In the myth of Ishtar's descent to the world of the dead, the goddess throws herself in a rage at Ereshkigal, goddess of the underworld. Ereshkigal responds by ordering her arrest and imprisonment:

Ereshkigal opened her mouth and spoke,
To Namtar, her messenger, she addressed herself:
"Go Namtar, imprison her in my palace."[1]

Ishtar is apprehended and imprisoned in the palace of Ereshkigal.

So as the mystery replayed, the woman who acted as Ishtar's avatar was apprehended and arrested. And it was that apprehension and that arrest that would trigger the riot and the movement that would alter world culture.

The Igniter

It happened as the police were making arrests of the patrons inside the bar, then taking them outside to the police wagon as the crowd outside stood watching. They brought out the woman with masculine features, the avatar, in handcuffs. According to eyewitnesses, she was fierce, violently fighting with at least four of the police officers as she shouted, protested her treatment, and cursed at them. The fighting was said to have lasted for about ten minutes.

It was then that she shouted to the crowd the words that would spark the uprising and the movement:

Why don't you guys do something?[2]

She was then heaved into the back of the police wagon. *It was at that moment that everything changed—and it all began.*

The Avengers

In the myth of Ishtar's descent, it was the goddess's disappearance, her apprehension, and her imprisonment that led to the issuing of the appeal and call to release her. The call would be answered, depending on the version of the myth, by the kurgarra, the galatur, or the assinnu. They were all intersexual beings. And their names were given to the goddess's priesthood, which included men dressed as women, men who had sexual relations with other men, male prostitutes, feminized men.

So on the night of Stonewall, it was the apprehending and arrest of the goddess's avatar, the raging woman, that would produce the call to action. And those who would answer that call and rise up in the angered frenzy that became the Stonewall riots would be intersexual or cross-gendered individuals. They would include males dressed as females, males who had sexual relations with other males, male prostitutes, feminized men—as were the priests of the goddess, the kurgarra, the galatur, and the assinnu, each of whom bore the name of the beings that came to her rescue in her imprisonment.

The Cursed

The myth identifies another characteristic or people group. Upon Ishtar's return from the dead, the intersexual beings that came to her aid are cursed for doing so. The curse is invoked by Ereshkigal. It was this:

> The sewers of the city shall be your drink,
> The shadow of the wall shall be your station,
> The threshold shall be your habitation,
> The besotted and the thirsty shall strike your cheek![3]

In other words, they would live in the city as impoverished and homeless. They would dwell in the shadow of the city wall. So the other segment, or characteristic, of those who took part in the uprising was *the homeless*. They were the homeless male prostitutes, who took refuge at Stonewall—they dwelled *in the shadow of the wall*. And they too would play a leading role in beginning the riots.

They Tear Away the Wife

In the myth of her return, the goddess is accompanied by demonic entities. They are described as having an agenda to separate man and woman, husband and wife, breaking apart marriage and family:

> They tear away the wife from a man's embrace. They snatch the son from a man's knee....They take the wife away from a man's embrace.[4]

So the goddess's most dramatic return to the world would be joined to the spirits that separated man from woman and woman from man and that would work toward the deconstruction of marriage and the disintegration of family.

The Moment of Frenzy

As the fighting woman was put into the police wagon, a spirit took hold of the crowd and turned it into an angry mob. The situation quickly turned dangerous, and the crowd, in the accounts of eyewitnesses, went berserk.

Who was the avatar? Who was the woman who incited the crowd and sparked the movement and everything that would follow? There is only one serious contender, a woman identified by name by several eyewitnesses. Though her later recollections were not always consistent, she would confide in and acknowledge to others that she was indeed the one. She was definitely at Stonewall that night and definitely fought back against the police. Whether she was the woman or one of them, she became the face of that resistance, the one who, in the mythology of Stonewall, sparked the uprising.

Protector of the Alehouse

In view of all this, her profile is striking. Like the goddess, she had masculine attributes. She was a male impersonator. Like the goddess, she was a fierce fighter. The goddess was the patron of the eshdam, the protector of the alehouse. So the woman believed to have sparked the Stonewall uprising would become known for serving as a protector of the alehouse. She would work as a bouncer for the lesbian bars of Greenwich Village. She would patrol the streets of the village as their guardian.

Charging Storm

Ishtar was the goddess of storms. The storm exemplified her nature, unpredictable, fiery, violent—stormy. Her roar was like thunder, her destructiveness like lightning. Ancient Sumerian and Akkadian writings joining the goddess to the storm are numerous:

> You charge forward like a charging storm. You roar with the roaring storm, you continually thunder...[5]

When the goddess displayed her power or her anger or entered into war, she did so as a raging storm:

> She brought out magnificent battle and called up a great storm.[6]

...covered in storm and flood, great lady Inana [*Ishtar*]...you destroy mighty lands with arrow and strength and overpower lands.[7]

You kept on attacking like an attacking storm,
Kept on blowing (louder) than the howling storm,
Kept on thundering (louder)...[8]

Loud Thundering Storm

The identification of the goddess with the storm is so strong that in an ancient Mesopotamian hymn, she is herself addressed as a storm:

Loud Thundering Storm...Proud Queen of the earth gods, supreme among the heaven gods, Loud Thundering Storm... You make the heavens tremble and the earth quake. Great Priestess, who can soothe your troubled heart? You flash like lightning over the highlands; you throw your firebrands across the earth.[9]

So the goddess was given the title Storm. And at Stonewall she would live up to it as she displayed her power, her anger and fury, and she entered into battle as a raging storm.

So what was the name of the one who served as her avatar that night? The name of the one who became known for sparking the riots and the movement that came from Stonewall was unique—her name was *Stormé*.

Both the goddess and her avatar bore the name *Storm*.

The Storm Unleashed

So the Stonewall uprising and the movement that would trace itself to that uprising were ignited by a female with male attributes, a fighter, a protector of alehouses, a fierce, angry, raging leader of those who crossed the boundaries of gender, the inciter of a multitude of feminized men—a mysterious figure known as *Stormé*. Was it the goddess, or was it her avatar? That night it made no difference. It was both. They acted as one.

Ishtar had returned. The same spirit that took hold of the multitude at Stonewall would, in time, take hold of millions. It all began that night when she set in motion a disturbance and a movement that would transform world culture.

She would unleash a storm.

◆◆◆

In the midst of the fury and violence of the uprising, a strange thing happened. To an objective observer it would have made no sense. But it too was part of the ancient mystery.

It was the Dance of the Goddess.

Chapter 40

The Dance of the Goddess

O NE OF THE strangest concepts in the lore of the goddess is summed up in the phrase *the Dance of Ishtar*. The strange thing about it is what it signified—war and destruction. It was a peculiar juxtaposition: the image of a dancing goddess against a backdrop of carnage, death, and devastation. An ancient inscription invokes the concept:

> ...fiery glow that blazes against the enemy, who wreaks destruction on the fierce, Dancing One, Ishtar, who masses the multitude...[1]

The Dance of Ishtar

On the opening night of the Stonewall riots, a strange thing happened. In the midst of the uprising, fighting, several of those involved began performing a dance. It was a bizarre convergence of music and dance performance on one hand, violence and destruction on the other. It was the Dance of Ishtar.

In ancient Mesopotamia it was not only the goddess who bore the title of the Dancing One. Her priests, the assinnu, were also known for their dances. So in the midst of the Stonewall uprising, Ishtar's modern-day assinnu performed a dance.

It was also the ministry of the ancient assinnu to sing the goddess's sacred songs. So those who danced at Stonewall also sang a song. As the ancient assinnu would sing their songs in the female dialect as if they were women, so their modern counterparts at Stonewall likewise sang their song and danced as if they were women.

Lovely Locks, Joy Girls, and Harlots

When Ishtar stood on the city wall and called down curses on Gilgamesh, she summoned her female ministers that they might share in her anguish. Three different kinds of women are mentioned in the account. One translation renders them as the "(cultic women) of lovely-locks, joy-girls, and harlots."[2] All three were associated with prostitution. The first of the three mentioned was known in the original language as the kezertu.

The kezertu were closely joined to Ishtar. The goddess's home city, Uruk, was known as the city of kezertu. They served in Ishtar's temples, and aside from their association with prostitution, the kezertu were known for making music. An ancient Sumerian tablet speaks of a girl who

> ...acted like a kezertu—*sang songs* and *played games.*[3]

The kezertu, one writer observes,

> ...would be involved in a variety of tasks, including *singing,* playing instruments, *dancing...*[4]

The Kezertu—They Who Wear Their Hair in Curls

Another writer notes of the kezertu,

> The women have distinctive hair-dos, sing songs, and dance in cultic performances.[5]

Accordingly, the kezertu were especially ordained to sing the songs and dance the dances of Ishtar. As for their "distinctive hair-dos," the reason the earlier-cited translation rendered the kezertu as the "*lovely locks*" is because of the word *kezertu* itself. *Kezertu* comes from the root word *kezeru*, which means *to curl one's hair.* So *kezertu* most specifically translates to and speaks of the women of Ishtar's cult who *wore their hair in curls.*

The Dancing Girls

On the opening night of the Stonewall riots, accompanying the goddess's manifestation was the manifestation of the kezertu. In some translations of the *Epic of Gilgamesh*, Ishtar's summoning of the kezertu is rendered this way:

> Ishtar called together her people, *the dancing and singing girls.*[6]

Her "dancing and singing girls" is another translation of *kezertu.* On the night of Stonewall, the goddess again called together her "dancing and singing girls."

Those engaged in the dance had no idea. But it was as if the spirit of the kezertu had taken them over. They were men, but now they became as women, dancing women, singing girls. Their song was a lewd taunt of the police officers. But the lyrics were most significant. They began,

> We are the Stonewall girls.[7]

And then came the words that stretched back to the Akkadian of ancient Mesopotamia and to the goddess; they sang,

> We *wear our hair in curls.*[8]

In the Akkadian tongue it was equivalent to saying,

> We are the kezertu.

And so it was that on the night of Stonewall, with the return of the goddess, the kezertu, the dancing girls who wore their hair in curls, also returned.

And as the Dance of Ishtar went on, the crowd was driven into a frenzy. It was now that the riot became so dangerous that the police retreated and barricaded themselves inside the bar. At that the spirit of the goddess grew even more furious. The elements of the ancient mystery were converging, the dance of the goddess was coalescing with battle and destruction.

I Shall Smash the Door

The goddess and her people were locked out of Stonewall. But this was the goddess who refused to be kept out of any realm because of a closed gate or locked door. Her ancient inscriptions describe her threats to bring violence against the gates and doors that would not open to her:

> If you do not open the gate for me to come in, I shall smash the door and shatter the bolt, I shall smash the doorpost and overturn the doors.[9]

The goddess had come to the gate of America. Now she would smash in the door. Possessed by her spirit, the mob began pounding and pummeling the bar's front door, attempting to shatter, smash, and break it open to get to the police officers inside. Stonewall was her dwelling place, her eshdam. She would not be locked out.

Lady of Fire

Ishtar was also the goddess of fire. An ancient hymn celebrates her use of the element to bring destruction in battle:

> Raining blazing fire down upon the Land...
> Lady who rides upon a beast...
> Destroyer of the foreign lands,
> You confer strength on the storm...
> Their great gateways are set afire.[10]

So now, inflamed by the "lady of fire," the crowd attempted to light the bar on fire with the police inside. They squirted lighter fluid through the openings in the doorway and threw burning pieces of garbage, lighted projectiles, and firebombs toward the police officers. They doused the front door with lighter fluid and set it on fire as well. One eyewitness summed up the intent of the mob with four simple words: "they wanted to kill."[11]

Some would consider it strange that such things as made up Stonewall would from that day forward be celebrated throughout the world, but even that goes back to the ancient mystery. The goddess's works of fire, destruction, and fury were likewise celebrated by her worshippers and lauded in her hymns.

Signs of the Goddess

That night, the signs of the goddess converged upon each other: the gate, the eshdam, the stone wall, the prostitutes, the cross-dressers, the homeless, the revived assinnu, the lion's head, the raging avatar named Stormé, the arresting, the call to help and its response, the kezertu, the dance of the goddess, the battle, the smashing of the door, the employing of fire, the fury, and the storm.

The goddess had returned. The door she had violently pounded that night appeared only to be that of a bar but was the door of a civilization that had been closed to her. She had now forced it open.

She would not rest or cease from her pounding until all the doors of Western civilization were likewise forced open to her. And with the door opened, the other gods and spirits, cast out in ancient times, would likewise return.

———————◆◆◆———————

We have seen how the place of the explosion and of the goddess's return, the city, the ground, and the very site of Stonewall were all determined by the ancient mystery. It *had* to happen where it happened. But what about its timing?

Beyond where it happened, could there be an ancient mystery that determined *when* it happened? In other words, did it happen when it *had* to happen?

Could the timing of the explosion at Stonewall have been determined by an ancient mystery involving the moon, the sun, the ancient calendar of Babylon, and the casting of an incantation?

Chapter 41

The Moon, the Sun, and the Spell

COULD THE TIMING of the explosion at Stonewall have been determined by a mystery from ages past involving the moon, the sun, the ancient calendar of Babylon, and the casting of an incantation?

The Time of Passion and Anguish

Ishtar's lover was the shepherd Tammuz. One day Tammuz offended her. The goddess set a horde of demons upon him. He tried to flee, but they caught up with him and brought him down to the land of the dead. After his departure the goddess, in remorse, began mourning him. Her sorrow and anguish were so great that nature itself stopped bearing life. Her maidens mourned with her. Finally, she descended to the land of the dead and brought him back to the world of the living, where he could dwell for part of the year before returning to the dead.

When were the days of Ishtar's mourning and anguish? They were days of summer. It was then that the Middle Eastern earth dried up and the leaves and fruit withered away—the sign of Tammuz's death and the separation of the two lovers.

The Days of Tammuz

But it was more specific than that. The days of Ishtar's sorrow fell within a specific month. The month was so closely connected to the goddess and her cult that it bore the name of her lover. It was the month of *Tammuz*.

The month of Tammuz was especially joined to the mythological realm. It marked the capture of the goddess's lover, his death, his descent and dwelling in the land of the dead. It was the month when the two gods were separated from each other. For the goddess, it was the month of unfulfilled longings, unanswered passions, and desires denied. It was the month of the goddess's sorrows, her longings and desires, her frustrations, her tears and anguish.

When did Stonewall take place?

It happened in the ancient month of Tammuz.

It was all part of the mystery of the gods that what happened at Stonewall took place in the ancient month of Tammuz. It was no accident that

Ishtar's return should take place in the month named after her lover and so deeply interwoven with her worship. Nor was it an accident that the replaying of her mythology at Stonewall should happen in the month most saturated with her mythology.

If the frustration and anguish that exploded into Stonewall were driven by the spirit of the goddess, then it is all the more striking that it happened during the very days devoted to her anguish and frustration. She was separated from and denied the object of her desires. The month's very name, Tammuz, stood for the denied object of her desires. So the days of Stonewall were the days of Tammuz, and the uprising was likewise born of frustration and the denial of desire.

The Descending of the Sun

In 1969 the month of Tammuz commenced on June 17, eleven days from Stonewall. One of the most important days on the calendar of the gods and the pagan world was that of the summer solstice—when the sun begins its annual descent. It was a time of rituals, worship, and sacrifices. The summer solstice was one of the most highly charged times of the pagan year. And in the case of Ishtar, the sun's descent paralleled the descent of her lover Tammuz into the underworld. In 1969 the sun began its annual descent on June 21. It was just days before the events that would set everything in motion, and exactly seven days to Stonewall.

Daughter of the Moon and the Fifteenth Day

Ishtar was strongly connected to the moon. In several of her mythologies her father is identified as the moon god. She herself was known as the *First Daughter of the Moon*. Since the Mesopotamian and Middle Eastern calendars were lunar based, each month began with the new moon, which reached its fullness around the fifteenth day, the month's center point, the day of its full moon. In the Babylonian world it was a holy day called the *Shapatu*. Ishtar was called "she of the fifteenth day, the mother of the month."[1]

In 1969 the month of Tammuz, the month of Ishtar's passion, came to its full moon on the weekend that began on June 27 and ended on June 29. It was the weekend of Stonewall. The riots began just before the full moon and continued just after it. The Stonewall riots centered on the full moon and center point of Tammuz.

It was no accident that the movement that would alter the lines of sexuality and gender was birthed in the month named after the lover of the goddess who altered the lines of sexuality and gender. And the days of that birth would cluster around the full moon of that month.

The Separation of Man and Woman

Tammuz was the month of the separation of Tammuz and Ishtar—the month that separated the male and the female. Thus the movement that would promote a sexuality in which male was separated from female and female separated from male was born in the month that separated the male from the female and the female from the male. The movement would advance and celebrate the turning of men away from women and the turning of women away from men.

The Spell

The day that sealed Stonewall and all that would come from it was June 26, 1969. It was then that deputy police inspector Seymour Pine obtained search warrant number 578. That was the definitive act that would set in motion the raid that would spark the riots, the uprising, and then the movement. It was in that one act that everything was sealed.

When was it? When was the warrant issued and the event that would become Stonewall sealed? On the ancient Mesopotamian and biblical calendar, it took place on the tenth day of the month of Tammuz. Is there any significance to that day? There is. An ancient Babylonian text reveals it. The tenth of Tammuz is the day given to perform the spell to cause

a man to love a man.[2]

So the day that would seal Stonewall and launch the movement that would come of it was not only one of the days of Tammuz and Ishtar but the specific day ordained from ancient times to cast a spell to make *a man love a man.*

The month of Tammuz, the full moon, the summer solstice, the separation of male and female, the days of frustration and anguish, and the day of the ancient spell to cause a man to love a man had all come together in the summer of 1969 to prepare the way for a goddess and to ignite an explosion.

It was the beginning. What happened at Stonewall would rapidly begin radiating into the surrounding culture, sparking a movement and then a metamorphosis. It would act as a catalyst to the overturning of Christian civilization, the foundations of biblical morality, and the near universal standards that had undergirded most civilizations for most of recorded history. It would bring that which had inhabited the shadows into the mainstream and then into dominion.

But behind the metamorphosis, its spectacles, its signs and symbols, its landmarks and seminal events, its celebrations, rites, and sacraments were mysteries of ancient origins. Behind them all were the gods.

Those are the mysteries we will now uncover.

We begin with the festal processions of Sumer and the gates of Babylon.

Part IX:

DOMINION

Chapter 42

Processions of the Gods

T HE WALL HAVING been broken, the gate having been forced open, what happened at Stonewall would now begin radiating from Greenwich Village to the world.

The People of Sumer Parade Before You

In ancient times the goddess stood at the center of culture and the pinnacle of its religion. She would seek to do so again.

She would begin transforming the rage and violence of Stonewall into a movement. And as her ancient cult involved sacred events and annual commemoration, observances, and festivals, she would now turn the Stonewall uprising into a sacred event to be religiously commemorated annually with its own rituals, observances, and festivals.

In the ancient Middle East she was especially known as the goddess of parades and processions. The ancient hymn "The Holy One" begins:

The people of Sumer parade before you.
They play the sweet ala-drums before you.[1]

Her parades became a central part of Mesopotamian and Middle Eastern popular culture and at the same time were an intrinsic part of her cult and worship.

Therefore, we might expect that the spirit of Ishtar, upon its return, would seek to commemorate the Stonewall riots with processions and parades. And this is exactly what would happen.

The goddess would create a new ritual, a parade and celebration that would eventually become a central component of American and Western culture. At the same time, it would increasingly take on the aura of a religious festival.

The Stonewall Parade

Five months after Stonewall, gay activists met in Philadelphia and planned a march to commemorate the Stonewall uprising to take place the following summer in New York City. It was to be repeated every year on the last Sunday of June. Three other marches were planned for that same weekend, one in San Francisco, one in Chicago, one in Los Angeles on Hollywood Boulevard. They were to be protest marches and parades at the same time.

On June 28, 1970, the one-year anniversary of the Stonewall riots, the participants gathered in Greenwich Village near Stonewall to begin the Christopher Street Liberation Day March. The name was taken from the street on which riots erupted. Beginning with a few hundred participants, the march proceeded up Sixth Avenue, where it swelled to a few thousand before reaching its destination at Central Park.

As planned, the parade would be repeated every summer as an annual observance. With each passing year, more marches would be held in more cities across America, and then around the world. They would be called Gay Liberation Marches, then Gay Pride Parades, and then simply Pride Parades.

They all took place at the same time of the year to commemorate the uprising that brought them into existence. The first march in Los Angeles down Hollywood Boulevard was called the Christopher Street West Association Parade, to identify it as Stonewall's westward extension. And many of the Pride Parades and festivities in Europe were part of what was called the Christopher Street Day celebration. All the Pride Parades, marches, processions, and festivities had as their birthplace Stonewall. Could even this go back to an ancient mystery?

The Gate of Ishtar

The most famous entranceway leading into ancient Babylon was the Gate of Ishtar. It was the starting point of the city's Processional Way. The great Babylonian parades would begin at the gate, then proceed down a half-mile road of ornate walls adorned with painted images. The goddess presided as queen of the great Babylonian processions and parades and thus was the one who inaugurated them at her entranceway.

So too it was the goddess who inaugurated the processions and parades that would cover the modern world. They began at Stonewall, the ground of her manifesting. Stonewall was her modern-day entranceway, the gate against which she pounded until it opened. Stonewall was the modern world's Gate of Ishtar. So it was no accident that it would become the inauguration point and launching ground from which the parades of millions would begin. And so as in ancient times, the most ubiquitous of the modern world's parades was set in motion at the gate of the goddess.

Processional Way

The ancient parades begun at Ishtar's Gate made their way through the Processional Way to the Temple of Marduk, the city's central thoroughfare. So the parades inaugurated by the goddess in the late twentieth century began in New York City, a Babylon of modern times, and proceeded along the city's central thoroughfare. And as the processions of Ishtar began at the gate, so the Pride Parades began in New York City, the gate of America. They would then make their way through the central thoroughfares of the great cities of the modern world and then trickle down to the smaller ones.

Gate of the Two Arches

As the ancient parades of the goddess began at the city wall, so her modern parades began at that which was named after a wall, Stonewall. The ancient parades began at the gate bearing the goddess's name, an entranceway covered with bricks. The modern parades of Ishtar were inaugurated at Stonewall, the wall of which was, like the Gate of Ishtar, covered with bricks.

The gate of the goddess was made up of two brick-covered archways, a smaller and a greater. The Stonewall Inn, likewise, possessed two brick-covered archway entrances—a smaller and a greater. In fact, it was these arch entrances that the mob of the Stonewall riots sought to break open and go through. As in ancient times, the massive processions and parades of the goddess began at the wall and the brick-covered arches of her gate.

The Lion, the Bull, and the Dragon

The Gate of Ishtar was famous for its depictions of the lion, a symbol of the goddess. Thus the ancient processions began under the sign of the lion. The processions birthed at Stonewall also began under the sign of the lion in that the Lion's Head marked the site of the uprising that birthed the parades.

It was through the Ishtar Gate that the gods entered the city in the form of idols and images. The gate and walls of the Processional Way were adorned with symbols of the gods—lions, dragons, and bulls. The lion, as we have seen, represented Ishtar. The dragon represented the god Marduk, who, in Babylonian mythology, was a lover of Ishtar. In the Bible the dragon, of course, is also a symbol of Satan. And the bull was a symbol of the god Adad. In the land of the Canaanites, Adad was *Hadad*, and *Hadad* was *Baal*.

Gateway of the Gods

So the Gate of Ishtar was the entranceway, the portal through which the gods entered. Thus the question: Could the entrance of Ishtar at Stonewall, from which the modern processions were born, likewise serve as a portal, the gateway of the gods?

In ancient times Ishtar's parades would draw the people into her worship. So they would again. The celebrations were, in essence, spiritual and even religious in nature. In a panoply of music and color, American and Western culture were being entranced into the worship of the goddess.

◆◆◆

If behind the parades of Pride Month were the processions of the goddess, could the descriptions of the ancient pageants give us revelation into the spectacles of our day?

Chapter 43

Spectacles of the Enchanted

I F WE WERE back in ancient times and witnessed the parades of the goddess, what would we have seen? Do we have any idea? We do.

Parade of the Goddess

The ancient writings of Mesopotamia describe them:

> The people of Sumer parade before you.
> I say, "Hail!" to Inanna [Ishtar], Great Lady of Heaven!
> They beat the holy drum and timpani before you....
> They play the holy harp and timpani before you.
> The people of Sumer parade before you.[1]

Ishtar's parades involved harps and drums, music and rhythm. They could be somber or even anguish-filled processions, or loud, festive, and celebratory pageants. The parades were known for something else—the bending of gender:

> The people of Sumer parade before you.
> The women adorn their right side with men's clothing.
> The people of Sumer parade before you....
> The men adorn their left side with women's clothing.[2]

The parades of the goddess featured men dressed as women, women dressed as men, each dressed as both, male priests parading as women, and cultic women acting as men. They were public pageants and spectacles of the transgendered, the cross-dressed, the homosexual, the intersexual, the cross-gendered.

The Return of the Mesopotamian Parade

If the goddess was to return to the modern world and to Western civilization, what would happen? Could the processions of the goddess return as well? Could her parades of the cross-gendered, of the androgynous, the homosexual, the transsexual, of men dressing as women, and women dressing as men—could they manifest again in the modern world?

181

The mystery would ordain that they would.

And that is exactly what would happen. The return of the goddess to Stonewall inaugurated the return of her ancient parades. After nearly two thousand years the goddess-inhabited processions of the cross-gendered begin reappearing on the urban streets of the modern world. Once they were seen in the streets of Uruk, Akkad, and Babylon. Now they would manifest in the streets of New York, London, and Paris.

The Pride Parades were resurrections of the goddess's ancient cultic parades.

Pageants of the Cross-Gendered

Even a modern transgendered commentator, writing of the goddess's ancient festival, could not fail to see the connection:

> The description of the festival appears to show the people of the city cross-dressing specifically for the purpose of the celebration. Indeed the whole thing sounds very like a gay pride parade.[3]

One paper on ancient views of sexuality, citing the processions of the goddess, notes that her cross-gendered participants

> ...took part in public processions, singing, dancing, wearing costumes, sometimes wearing women's clothes and carrying female symbols.[4]

So the Pride Parades would involve the same elements: singing, dancing, costumes, men wearing women's clothing and carrying female symbols.

Men of Colored Fabrics

An ancient Sumerian inscription says this of the participants in the goddess's processions:

> The male prostitutes comb their hair before you.
> They decorate the napes of their necks with colored scarfs.[5]

A modern commentary on the inscription says this:

> In order to look more like a woman, some of these homosexual priests let their hair grow long, and then after "tightening

their hairgrips for her, male prostitutes [would] parade before her, holy Inana [Ishtar]. Their locks of hair at the back are adorned for her with coloured rags."[6]

The mention of both cross-gendered men and colored cloths is also striking, as both elements describe the modern Pride Parades. The prominent use of colored fabrics can be found in the clothing, signs, and flags displayed in the processions.

Carnivals of Pride

The goddess's ancient parade is described by one Mesopotamian scholar as

...a carnival-like procession.[7]

So the Pride Parades of modern time, though born of protest, had likewise evolved into *carnival-like processions*. The writer goes on to describe other aspects of the ancient processions:

Not only do the people parade playing musical instruments but also costumed asexual or hermaphrodite personnel, transvestites, wearing male attire on their right side and female attired on their left...[8]

One can see each of these elements present in some way in the modern Pride Parades. The label *pride* itself is unwittingly connected to the goddess. Pride was central to her nature. One of her hymns addresses her as

...the impetuous lady, *proud* among the Anuna gods....full of *pride*...[9]

Muddy Paints, Artful Eyes, and Purple Stripes

In his novel, *Metamorphoses,* the second-century Roman writer Apuleius gives a glimpse into the spectacle that would attend the goddess's parades as he describes the trappings of the related ancient male priesthood of the *galli:*

The following day they went out, wearing various colored undergarments with turbans and saffron robes and linen garments thrown over them, and everyone hideously made up, their faces crazy with muddy paints and their eyes artfully lined. Some wore tunics, fastened with belts, with purple stripes flowing in every direction like spears and yellow shoes on their feet.[10]

Again, we see the spectacle of men publicly displaying themselves as women and adorning themselves with colored fabrics. Apuleius' description also includes the mention of eyeliner and heavily exaggerated makeup. These too have become defining elements of the modern Pride Parade in its prominent displaying of transvestites, female impersonators, and drag queens.

The Footsteps of Her Priests

The goddess's parades were known for flouting societal norms and the distinctions of gender. Her modern parades would be known for doing the same. Descriptions of the ancient processions include such adjectives as *licentious*, *bawdy*, *unbridled*, and *lewd*. The same words would be used to describe their modern incarnations.

Through the Pride Parades the goddess would bring her flouting of convention into the modern world. She would use them to pound open the last closed doors of Western civilization.

Millions of people around the world were now partaking in the goddess's revived processions just as her priests and cultic personnel had done in ancient times.

Millions were now walking in the footsteps of her ancient priests and becoming her servants.

◆◆◆

It was not only men who took part in the goddess's processions but women. Their presence is another component of the mystery and the return that is now affecting our world. Its opening will take us from the islands of Greece to the streets of ancient Sumer, and from one of the goddess's most famous incarnations to a dance of swords.

Chapter 44

The Purple Garland and the Double-Edged Axe

COULD THE ROLE that women played in the processions of the goddess reveal another side of the mystery?

The Women of the Goddess

Women not only took part in the goddess's parades but also displayed her power to blur, break, and switch the lines of gender, but from the other side. As the parading men assumed traditionally female roles, the parading women assumed traditionally male roles.

It is never explicitly spoken, but the idea of lesbianism was always implicit. If under Ishtar's power women could take on the roles and functions of men, then taken to its ultimate conclusion, that would include the role and function of husband or lover.

It was implicit in Ishtar's androgyny. In nature, temperament, and role, she was as masculine as she was feminine. She transformed herself from female to male and back again. This, again, would imply the altering of her desire. So though it was never overt, lesbianism was always implicit in the goddess's crossing of gender and sexuality.

It was there, as well, among Stonewall's patrons. Though making up a small component, women were among them. It was there the night it all began when a lesbian in handcuffs incited the uprising against the police. And it was there afterward in the Gay Pride Parades, where lesbians made up a large part of the participants.

Sign of the Two Ishtars

But could there be more that joins the modern revival of lesbianism to the ancient goddess?

Among the most basic modern representations of lesbianism is that of two crosses topped with two large circles intertwined with each other—two symbols of the female joined to each other. How did the female symbol originate? Its first known appearance in that context is found in the works of the Swedish botanist Carl Linnaeus in the eighteenth century. He used it to represent female flowers.

Linnaeus took the symbol from the Greeks, who used it to represent the metal copper, which was associated with the planet Venus. The planet was associated with the goddess Venus. Venus was the Roman incarnation of the Greek Aphrodite, and Aphrodite, the Greek incarnation of Ishtar. Thus the sign that, to this day, represents the female, known as the "Venus symbol," ultimately goes back to Ishtar. And thus the symbol for lesbianism, based on the symbol of Venus, likewise goes back to the goddess. The sign is, in effect, that of two Venuses, two goddesses, two Ishtars intertwined with each other.

Sappho and the Terrible Enchantress

The modern revival of lesbianism takes inspiration from the Greek poet Sappho. Sappho led a *thiasos*, a community of young women for which she served as teacher. Her sexuality is, to this day, a matter of debate, but her writings appear to indicate a romantic or erotic attraction to women.

The patron deity protecting Sappho's community was the goddess Aphrodite—the Greek incarnation of Ishtar. Sappho worshipped the goddess and wrote of being intimately acquainted with her. Her poetry is filled with elements from the goddess's cult, rites, and worship.

Only one of Sappho's poems still exists in its entirety. It is a prayer to Aphrodite, whom she addresses as the *"terrible enchantress."*[1] Prominent in Ishtar's cult were prayers to the goddess entreating her to use her magic to alter the affections of others. That, in effect, was Sappho's prayer. But the object of her affection is a woman. In the poem the goddess appears to Sappho and assures her that she will cause the woman to love her.

Sappho was born on the Greek island of Lesbos. From the name of that island comes the word *lesbian*. Thus behind the word *lesbian* is the island of Lesbos. Behind Lesbos is Sappho. Behind Sappho is Aphrodite. And behind Aphrodite is Ishtar. It all goes back to Ishtar.

The Violet-Crowned Goddess

It is from Sappho and the island of Lesbos, as well, that the colors purple and violet and, from this, lavender, have become associated with lesbianism. Her poetry is adorned with mentions of purple or violet.

It is from Sappho, as well, that the violet became the symbolic flower of lesbianism. She writes more than once of a woman crowned with a garland of violets. Even in this is the goddess. Aphrodite was *"the violet-crowned"* goddess.[2] Thus even the colors and flower of lesbianism went back to the ancient goddess, the incarnation of Ishtar.

The Double-Edged Axe

In the 1970s a symbol was adopted by the emerging lesbian movement. It was the most prominent of the movement's first symbols. In 1999 the symbol was incorporated into a flag of purple that was to be used as a banner to represent the movement and lesbianism itself.

The symbol was an axe with two blades—the double-edged axe, also known as the *labrys*. Why was it chosen to be the sign of lesbianism? It goes back to ancient times. On the island of Crete the double-edged axe was a sacred symbol of the ancient Minoan religion. The symbol was associated with women. In the days of the Roman Empire the double-edged axe was associated with the mythological warrior women known as the Amazons.

The double-edged axe, as a symbol of women independent of men and taking on the nature and place of men, was thus chosen as a modern symbol of lesbianism. The ancient axe became part of Gay Pride Parades, displayed on banners carried by those who saw themselves as heirs to the ancient Amazons.

Weapon of the Priestess

But the double-edged axe, and its connection to the altering of gender, goes back beyond the people of Greece and Crete. It is found in the writings of ancient Mesopotamia, in the city of Sumer. It appears in a hymn to the goddess. It is from an inscription we have already seen—the describing of the goddess's parades: the male prostitutes, the men parading as women, the male and female transvestites, the cross-gendered, the sound of drums, and the colored fabrics. It says this:

> The people of Sumer parade before you....
> The young men, who carry hoops, sing to you.[3]

The carrying of hoops was associated with women. The young men are feminized. But it goes on:

> The maidens and coiffured priestesses walk before you,
> They carry the sword.[4]

The young women and priestesses, on the other hand, are carrying objects associated with men. They are the goddess's women who, following in her footsteps, take on the roles of men. As the goddess brandishes a sword in battle, so do the women of her parade. But according to the account, the women brandish another object as well:

They carry the...double-edged axe.[5]

Hymns, Banners, and Spirits

So it is in an ancient hymn to the goddess that the double-edged axe makes its appearance. And the context of its appearance is that of women taking on the functions of men. And beyond that they take up the axe in the gender-crossing parade of the goddess. And now, in the modern world, the same object from Ishtar's processions was revived to serve as the symbol of lesbianism, women taking on the roles and functions of men.

So the same weapon wielded by women in the ancient world to bend the lines of gender and sexuality now became the symbol of women in the modern world bending the lines of gender and sexuality.

And as gender-crossing women lifted up the double-edged axe as they marched in the goddess's ancient gender-bending parades, now they would lift up banners emblazoned with the image of the very same axe as they marched in the modern gender-crossing parades of their revival.

The women had no idea they were replaying an ancient mystery. But the spirits have their own way.

◆◆◆

We saw in Stonewall how the mythic functions of the Babylonian calendar converged to determine the exact timing of the uprising. But the mystery of timing would not end on Christopher Street.

It would spread into the mainstream culture until the world's yearly cycle was imprinted by it. Yet few in the modern world could have imagined that the calendar in which they lived their lives had been changed by a mystery that went back to ancient Mesopotamia and that was connected to mythology and the workings of the gods.

To uncover the mystery, we must go back to the pagan celebrations of ancient Phoenicia and the Latin writings of the early church father known as *Saint Jerome*.

Chapter 45

Junium

THERE WAS ONE time of the year especially indwelled by the goddess.

The Month of Her Possession

Ishtar played a part in other holy days and festivals, but it was this one time of year that her mythology, her passions, her frustration and anguish, her desires and longings, her rituals, and her possession of multitudes saturated Mesopotamian culture for an entire month. It was during those days that her spirit seemed everywhere.

It was then that the people of Mesopotamia not only worshipped her but, in their passions, became *as* her. They cried out for her lover Tammuz as if it were her crying out through them. They yearned as if it were her yearning in them. They moved in procession as if it were her moving in procession. So the prophet Ezekiel was given a vision in which he saw the women of Israel weeping, as if it were Ishtar weeping for Tammuz. The people became her channels. The goddess of possession possessed them.

It was at that time of year that her mythology exerted an amplified power to infiltrate daily life. They were the days when, according to her mythology, she and Tammuz were separated. He was in the underworld, the land of the dead, and she was in the land of the living, seeking to be reunited. Rituals, observances, festivals, and processions dedicated to the goddess and the object of her desire took place throughout the Middle East. One could hardly escape it. During those days, the air was especially filled with her presence.

The Twenty-Nine Days

What would happen if the goddess returned to the modern world? Would she again mark out and lay claim to a similar time of year? Would she again create rituals to be performed during that time, observances to be kept, festivals to be celebrated, and processions to be followed? And would her spirit again especially indwell those days?

The answer is *yes*. That is exactly what she would do. Upon her return to Western civilization, the goddess set out to mark and lay claim to a space of time every year as her own, a time that her spirit could especially inhabit. As she was the goddess of pride, the time would be crowned with the name *pride*.

The time of the goddess and the object of her passions lasted approximately twenty-nine days. So one month of the ancient Middle Eastern calendar was especially given for the possession of the goddess, her lover, and her mythology. Rites, festivals, and processions took place from the month's opening to its last day.

So the mystery would ordain that the spirit of the goddess would again seek to lay claim to a similar space of time in modern times, *one month each year* on the calendar of the civilization she was now seeking to possess.

And so it happened in exact accordance with the ancient mystery.

The Sacred Month

In the wake of Stonewall, gay activists established marches and parades to celebrate homosexuality and then an entire week, Gay Pride Week. But in ancient times the goddess laid claim to an entire month of observances and parades. And so Gay Pride Week was then transformed into Gay Pride Month.

To increase its acceptability and further popularize it, its name would later be shortened to *Pride Month*. So as in ancient times, the spirit of the goddess was given an entire month to indwell and possess. And as in ancient times, that month would be known for its processions and parades, observances, rituals, and the increase of her power.

It was a strange phenomenon. The celebrating of that which once occupied the forbidden corners of society had come to permeate and dominate American and Western culture.

America and other nations of the West were now devoting an entire month to honor, praise, and celebrate a form of sexuality that a little while earlier had been nearly universally viewed as a form of immorality. Now it was being treated as sacred.

A Strange Veneration

Equally strange, nations were placing the celebration of this mode of sexuality above their own holidays. Nations would typically devote a day to the celebration of their birth or independence. But they were now devoting almost thirty times that amount of time in order to celebrate a particular form of sexuality.

And it was happening all over the world. Nations with little in common were now celebrating the same holiday, giving homage, veneration, and praise all to the same thing and to that which they had only a little while earlier deemed to be sin. What could account for such a strange and dramatic transformation? It was more than natural. It was the work of the gods.

In all of history, there had never been a phenomenon quite like it. And yet Pride Month was the resurrection of the ancient month of the goddess's possession. So now again, as in ancient times, an entire month was given to the indwelling of a spirit that blurred and broke the lines of gender, that feminized men and masculinized women, that turned the one into the other and caused them to be paraded in the city streets.

Finding Tammuz

When in the ancient year did the days of the goddess and her lover fall? They fell in the summer. It was the ancient month of Tammuz. Since it was based on the lunar cycle, its timing, with regard to the Western Gregorian calendar, would of course oscillate. Tammuz can begin in June or July. But 70 percent of the time it begins in June.

Jamieson, Fausset & Brown's Commentary on the Whole Bible, published in 1871, says this of the month and of its ancient celebrations:

> An annual feast was celebrated to him in *June* (hence called *Tammuz* in the Jewish calendar).[1]

The Bible commentator Joseph Benson, who lived in the eighteenth and early nineteenth century, wrote this of the month and its worship:

> *Tammuz*...which also is used for the tenth month, reckoning from the autumnal equinox, *that is, the month of June*; and *Tammuz*, as the object of worship, expresses the *solar light* in its perfection, as in the summer solstice.[2]

Benson brings out the link between the month of Tammuz and the summer solstice. There is only one month in which the summer solstice takes place each year—the month of June.

Junium

Saint Jerome, who lived in the Roman Empire at the time of its conversion from paganism to Christianity, was most famous for producing the Vulgate, the Latin translation of the Bible. But he was also known for writing biblical commentaries. One of these was on the Book of Ezekiel.

It was that book that contained the description of the Hebrew women, in the spirit of Ishtar, weeping for Tammuz. In commenting on the passage, Jerome drew from his knowledge of the observances, rituals, and practices that were still being performed at the time of his writing. His original words in Latin read:

> Quem nos Adonidem interpretati sumus, et Hebraeus et Syrus sermo Thamuz vocat...

> Adonis is called *Tammuz* both in Hebrew and Syria...

Then he writes of the god's death and the time of its occurrence:

> ...*in mense Junio*...*occisus.*[3]

> in *the month of June*...is killed.

So Jerome identifies the time of Tammuz's death as the *"mense Junio,"* the month of June. He continues:

> ...eumdem *Junium mensem eodem appellant nominee*, et *anniversariam ei celebrant* colemnitatem.[4]

> ...*they call this month of June by the same name*, and keep an *annual festival* in his honor.

Thus, according to Jerome and other observers of his day, the month of Tammuz was equivalent or most equivalent to *"Junium mensem," "this month of June."* Tammuz corresponds with Junium and Junium with Tammuz. June is also identified as the month in which the *annual festival* takes place. Thus the identification of Tammuz with June, and thus June as the month of the annual celebration linked to the goddess and her mythology, are ancient ones going back to the Romans, those who gave the month of June its name.

The Repossession of June

So if the goddess returned, what would happen to the month of her possession? The calendar of the modern world was based not on that of ancient Mesopotamia or the Middle East but on that of Rome. We might then expect that, of all months, she would choose the month of the summer solstice. We might expect that she would choose the month that, more than any other, inaugurated the days of Tammuz, her lover—*Junium mensem*—the month of June.

So she would take special possession of it. She would turn June into the time of her channeling. And since June had long been known as the time of weddings, the joining of man and woman, its modern transformation would be all the more dramatic.

And thus June became Pride Month, and Pride Month became June. As America and the West turned away from God and Christianity, the ancient month returned to the goddess. And as in ancient times, the summer solstice and the days it inaugurated marked the time of the goddess's processions and parades.

The Summer Liturgies

The festival of the summer month of which Jerome and others wrote involved rituals of lamentation and mourning over Tammuz's descent. We know that women were involved in those rituals. But it was not women alone. The assinnu, the kalu, and the gala, Ishtar's cross-gendered priesthood, the men who dressed as women, were given a central part in the rituals. They would lead the lamentations by chanting and wailing in the female dialect. So now, in the revived processions of June, men would again take on the attributes of women.

After nearly two thousand years, the month that Jerome called *Junium* had revived its pagan function as the vessel for *"the annual festival."* June would again serve the instrument of the goddess's power, the time when her spirit would especially possess the culture in which she dwelled.

Festival of Inversion

The month of Tammuz, or Junium, centered on the mythology of Ishtar and her lover. But it was not about their union. It was about their separation. It was about the obstruction of passion and desire. So the modern observances of June as the commemoration of the Stonewall riots were born of the same thing, frustration and anger over the obstruction of desire. The parades themselves were aimed at tearing down all walls of resistance and to remove the hindrances separating desire from its fulfillment.

Beyond this was a strange coming together of the goddess's observances. The timing of Pride Month hearkened back to the days when Tammuz and Ishtar were separated, and thus to the theme of separation—the separation of man from woman and woman from man. It was thus the perfect time for a celebration of homosexuality, lesbianism, and other alternate sexualities. But the revelry of Pride Month hearkened back to the goddess's celebratory festivals.

In Pride Month the two came together. The modern observance was not a lamentation over the separation of male and female—but a celebration. It was now a festival that *celebrated* the separation—a monthlong holiday that rejoiced in men separated from women and women separated from men. In this the rites of the goddess converged into a festival of inversion.

The Licentious Rites of Midsummer

And yet the ancient rites and festivals observed in the month of Tammuz's separation were also noted for their sexual licentiousness. One commentator writes this of the festival as practiced in ancient Phoenicia or Lebanon:

> The women of Gebal used to repair to this temple [*of Aphrodite/Ishtar*] in midsummer to celebrate the death of Adonis or Tammuz, and there arose in connection with this celebration those licentious rites.[5]

The writer places the licentious rights at *midsummer*, the summer solstice, in June. The second-century Syrian writer Lucian gives his own account of the rites and observances of June:

> I saw too at Byblos a large temple, sacred to the Byblian Aphrodite [*Ishtar*]: this is the scene of the secret rites of Adonis [*Tammuz*]...[6]

He goes on to describe how the women would shave their heads in homage to the slain god Adonis/Tammuz and that those who refused to do so had to offer their bodies to strangers as prostitutes and give the proceeds to the goddess as a sacrifice.

The early church historian Eusebius writes of the same temple of Venus/Aphrodite/Ishtar in Phoenicia on which the rites and processions of June were centered:

> ...the votaries of impurity...destroyed their bodies with effeminacy. Here men undeserving of the name forgot the dignity of their sex...here too unlawful commerce of women and adulterous intercourse, with other horrible and infamous practices...[7]

The Temple of Venus

The ending of the midsummer festival and processions of the goddess is implicit in the writings of the early church historians Eusebius and

Socrates Scholasticus. Both record the clearing away of the shrine of Venus, Aphrodite, Ishtar, in Lebanon by the Emperor Constantine:

> He likewise demolished the temple of Venus at Aphaca on Mount Libanus, and abolished the infamous deeds which were there celebrated.[8]

The temple, or shrine, of Venus at Aphaca on Mount Libanus served as the source of the festivals of which Saint Jerome wrote and identified with June. So the festivals of June, or Tammuz, came to an end.

Thus one of the most overlooked signs of the conversion of Western civilization to Christianity was the ending of monthlong celebrations of midsummer with its June parades and gender-crossing spectacles.

And thus the return of the monthlong celebration of midsummer, the revival of the June parades, and reappearance of the gender-crossing spectacles was not an accident. It was a sign of the de-Christianization of Western civilization and its subsequent re-paganization.

The temple of Venus was, ultimately, the temple of Ishtar. The ending of the June processions was linked to its destruction. And its destruction was linked to the exile of the goddess and the gods. So if the hallowing of June, the annual festival, the parades and processions of the cross-gendered, should return, it would be a sure sign not only of de-Christianization and re-paganization but of that which accompanies both—the return of the goddess, and the return of the gods.

The Return of Junium

For Christians of the first centuries, such as Eusebius, the rites of June and their associated practices could only be seen as celebrations of immorality. For Christians of the twentieth and twenty-first centuries, the revived rites of June and their related practices would be seen in the same way. They were not alone. Many others in ancient and modern times would view it similarly. For those not swept up in its fervor, June's transformation was a mystery.

The monthlong celebration seemed almost religious in nature. And it was. It was the return of an ancient religious observance. The "sacred" procession of June was not a strange phenomenon to pagan culture. The sight of parades in which men dressed as women and women as men and the distinctions of gender were blurred was, to pagan eyes, a familiar one.

Their return was the natural outcome of the re-paganization of Western civilization. What had begun with the turning away from God had now given birth to the rites and processions of the pagan summer festival.

The parades had vanished with the gods. Their disappearance was a sign that the gods had departed. The return of the parades was thus the sign of the opposite—the gods had returned. And the rising magnitude of the summer celebration was a sign of the rising power of the gods and the intensifying hold they were exerting on America and the world. The departure from God had allowed the pagan mystery month to rise from the dead. June was reverting to its pre-Christian state. Junium was returning.

Month of Apostasy

In the Bible the month of Tammuz is known for something else. It was in Tammuz that the nation of Israel first turned away from God and to the realm of gods and idols—to the golden calf. It was June that most often began that Hebrew month. And so now again, June would mark the turning away of another nation and another civilization from God and to the gods. It was the month of apostasy—that of a nation and that of a civilization.

What happened to June is another reminder that whenever a nation or civilization or, for that matter, a life turns away from God, it will never remain neutral. It will never stay empty. It will become indwelled by something else, something other than God. It will become inhabited by the gods. Those who had taken part in the removal of prayer and the Word from American public life could not have imagined what it would lead to. But the empty house could not stay empty. A civilization had turned away from its worship of God. Now the sacraments of a different worship had come in. The door was left open; the house was found empty; the spirits came in; the gods returned and with them, their holy days.

———◆◆◆———

Is it possible that behind a sign that now appears in everything from corporate logos, video games, and children's cartoons to T-shirts, coffee mugs, cereal boxes, and the flagpoles of American embassies—a sign lifted up by people of every background, by leaders and nations—lies an ancient deity?

And is it possible that this sign that now covers the world actually serves as an instrument of that deity to the accomplishing of purposes unknown to those who bear it?

Chapter 46

The Sign

ONE SIGN ABOVE all others has come to represent the movement that started at Stonewall—the sign of the rainbow.

The Rainbow Flag

The rainbow flag was designed by Gilbert Baker, an openly gay man and drag queen, and was first flown on June 25, 1978. In 1994 the sign of the rainbow was adopted as the official symbol of gay pride. It soon became the ubiquitous symbol of the movement and all it represented, flown and recognized all over the world.

But could even this be the manifestation of an ancient mystery? And could it go back to the gods?

The original rainbow flag had eight colors, each representing one of eight elements of the movement. One would have expected the colors of the flag to represent such things as liberation, tolerance, respect, empowerment, or different people groups. But the flag and the colors of the rainbow it bore represented that which was altogether different.

The flag was a representation of a strange assemblage of themes and elements that seemed to have little to do with one another. One would have been hard-pressed to find a common thread or unifying theme to bind them all together and make sense of it all. But there was a unifying theme and a common thread binding them all together—the goddess.

Pink

It goes without saying that Ishtar was the goddess of sex. She was the embodiment of passion, love, lust, sexual desire, and sexual practices in every form.

The first color of the original rainbow flag was pink. It represented sex.

Red

From Ishtar came life. She was the source of all fertility and procreation, the fruitfulness of the earth, of animals, and of humanity. She was the wellspring of all the generative powers of nature. When she was in the underworld, the generation of life came to a standstill. Ishtar was the goddess of life.

The second color of the rainbow flag was red. It represented life.

Orange

The preeminent Mesopotamian goddess of healing was named *Gula*. But in time Ishtar appropriated from her the powers of healing, and Gula fell into obscurity. Ancient inscriptions survive with prayers and prescriptions for healing addressed to or centered on Ishtar. She is the one of whom it is written *"takes sickness away."*[1] It is written that her effigy was once carried as far away as Egypt to heal an ailing Pharaoh.

The third color of the rainbow flag was orange. It represented healing.

Yellow

Ishtar was closely associated with the celestial lights. The morning and evening star would carry her name, Venus. And the moon was her father. But there was another celestial light that was intrinsically bound to her—the sun. The Assyrian sun god *was* named *Shamash,* the Akkadian word for sun. He was Ishtar's brother. Ishtar was, in fact, the sun's twin sister. So strong is her identification with the sun that we can find a sun disk at her side in many of her carved images.

The fourth color of the rainbow flag was yellow. It represented the light of the sun.

Green

Ishtar was, as were many of the pagan gods, an embodiment of nature. She represented the vital forces of nature, the fruitfulness of the earth, the rain, thunder, and storms of the heavens. She was among the prominent and central of all nature gods.

The fifth color of the rainbow flag was green. It represented nature.

Turquoise

As we have seen, Ishtar was deeply connected to the realm and practice of magic. Her name was especially invoked in the casting of spells and enchantments and what today would be known as the occult arts. She was the goddess of magic.

The sixth color of the rainbow flag was turquoise. It represented magic.

Indigo

Though Ishtar was the goddess of storms, on the other hand, because of it, it was to her altars that supplicants came entreating her to grant them serenity. An old Babylonian hymn says this:

> At her glance, serenity comes into being.[2]

The seventh color of the rainbow flag was indigo. It represented serenity.

Violet

And of course, Ishtar was a spirit, just as the gods were typically viewed by their worshippers as spirits. Beyond that, we have seen the connection of the gods to the spirits, the Hebrew *shedim* and the Greek *daemonia*.

Thus the last color of the rainbow flag is of special note—violet. It represents spirit. What kind of spirit is represented? The color violet was especially connected to Aphrodite, the *"violet-crowned goddess."* Aphrodite was, of course, an incarnation of Ishtar.

So the first color set the stage, as it represented sexuality. The last color summed it up. It represented a spirit—the spirit of sexuality—the very goddess known from ancient times as Ishtar.

Could there be more to the mystery?

Rainbow Ishtar

Ishtar was goddess of the sky, queen of heaven, master of tempests, hurler of lightning bolts, giver of rain. The ancient hymn praises her for it:

> Loud Thundering Storm, you pour your rain over all the lands and all the people.[3]

She controlled the storm. She directed its every gust, every peal of thunder, and every drop of rain. And thus the rainbow was under her lordship and direction.

There is an ancient Elamite inscription that reads *"Manzat Ishtar."* There is debate over whether the name *Ishtar* is to be taken just as it appears or as a generic noun. Nevertheless, the inscription translates to the name *Rainbow Ishtar*.

The Jewels of Heaven

In the *Epic of Gilgamesh*, in the wake of a colossal rain and deluge,

> Ishtar also came, she lifted her necklace with the jewels of heaven.[4]

The necklace with *the jewels of heaven* has long been understood as the rainbow. So in the aftermath of the storm, the goddess lifts the rainbow up into the sky. Thus Ishtar has been credited as the creator of the rainbow.

The Goddess With Rainbow Eyes

Then there is the strange description of the goddess as contained in an ancient Babylonian hymn of her praise:

> ...her eyes are multicolored and iridescent[5]

The eyes of the goddess are of multiple colors like the colors of the rainbow. The ancient word is translated as *iridescent*. *Iridescent* comes from the Latin root *iris*, which means rainbow. *Iris* is also the name of the Roman goddess of the rainbow. Thus the eyes of Ishtar are like rainbows.

As a Rainbow

And then there is the myth of the goddess and the gardener. A gardener plants a tree under which the goddess lies down and falls asleep. While the goddess is asleep, the gardener rapes her. When she awakes and realizes what has been done to her, she flies into a rage and begins sending down plagues on the earth. She then goes to her father to seek his help. He tells her where the gardener is hiding. She sets out to find him. How she sets out on her mission of vengeance is striking:

> She *stretched herself like a rainbow across the sky* and reached thereby as far as the earth.[6]

So in order to accomplish her mission against the one who violated her, the goddess stretches herself *like a rainbow across* the sky. The goddess becomes as the rainbow. The rainbow becomes her mode of action and being. It became the means by which she executed her will.

Ishtar is considered the first of the gods for whom we have written evidence. Her connection to the rainbow is most ancient, long preceding that of the Greek goddess Iris and others. She was joined to the rainbow from the very start, from the dawn of recorded history and mythology.

The Sign

So what would happen if the goddess returned? Would the rainbow also return as a sign of her power? It would. And it has. It was no accident that the movement that had been birthed by the goddess should take as its symbol the sign of the goddess. Those who designed it, those who carried it, and those who adopted it to serve as the defining symbol of the movement had no idea of the connection.

The movement that had crossed the boundaries of sexuality and altered the parameters of gender now adopted as its symbol the sign of the ancient goddess who had crossed the boundaries of sexuality and altered the parameters of gender.

The movement that had made June its sacred month of observances and processions was now covered with the sign of the goddess whose sacred month of observances and processions most often began in June. The goddess had marked her resurrected religion and worship with the sign of her ownership.

Banner of War

The goddess had stretched herself across the sky in order to punish her offender. The rainbow was a mode of war by which she exacted vengeance and judgment. So too behind the rainbow that began manifesting in the wake of Stonewall was an ancient goddess arming herself for battle. And it would be through that sign that her war would be waged.

Those who paraded with it, those who wore it on their clothing, those who raised it outside their office buildings, those who disseminated it on the internet, and those who placed it on their products had no idea of the spirit that lay behind it or of the end to which it led. Behind its flowing colors was a banner of war.

As in her ancient mythology, the rainbow would be the means and mode by which the goddess would again seek to exact vengeance on those whom she believed had wronged her—especially on those who had cast her out.

◆◆◆

Could a mystery that goes back to the temples of ancient Babylon actually be determining the cases, the workings, and even the rulings of the United States Supreme Court?

Chapter 47

Days of the Goddess

THE RITES OF the goddess were meticulously timed. They could only take place on the days appointed according to the Mesopotamian calendar. So as we have seen, the goddess's entrance and the inauguration of her resurrected movement at Stonewall took place at the exact time ordained by the Mesopotamian calendar and the ancient mystery.

According to the mystery, it took place in the month of Tammuz and, on the Western calendar, in the month of June. It was set in motion within days of the summer solstice and centered on the full moon of Tammuz, all linked to the goddess. It was all sealed on June 26, 1969, the tenth of Tammuz, the day that in the Babylonian calendar was ordained for the casting of spells to cause *"a man to love a man."*

But could there be even more to the mystery? Could it be that behind some of the most pivotal events of American culture lies the calendar of the goddess? And could their timing reveal her fingerprints?

The Tammuz Marches

Before Stonewall, there was a series of protests or pickets on behalf of homosexual rights known as the *Annual Reminder* or the *Reminder March*. The protests took place in Philadelphia by Independence Hall every year on Independence Day. They were small and, for the most part, ignored by the media. But after Stonewall, the Reminder March would be moved to New York City and would transform into the Pride Parade.

The first Reminder March took place in 1965 in the summer—in the ancient month of Tammuz. It fell on Tammuz 4. The second took place in 1966—also in the month of Tammuz—on Tammuz 16. The third, in 1967, took place within days of Tammuz. The fourth, in 1968, took place on Tammuz 8. And the fifth and last, in 1969, took place on Tammuz 18.

Thus 80 percent of those early marches took place in the month of the goddess and her lover Tammuz. All of them took place in or by Tammuz—the same month in which the Stonewall riots broke out.

But the Reminder Marches took place *before* Stonewall. The timing of the one had nothing to do with the other. The scheduling of the Reminder March was based on American history. The timing of Stonewall was based on a deputy police inspector's planned raid and an explosion that was planned by no one. Yet they both fell in the ancient Mesopotamian month connected to the goddess.

Beyond that, the first Reminder March took place on an ancient Mesopotamian holy day connected to the ceremonial funeral of the goddess's lover. So did another. A third took place on another ancient Mesopotamian holy day, this one appointed for a ceremonial procession in honor of Ishtar's lover.

Toward the End of June

Then came Stonewall, and from Stonewall, the days and weeks and then months of Pride. All these would take place, as we have noted, in June, the month that, more than any other, began the observances and celebrations of Tammuz.

But the timing was more specific. In his seminal work, *Tammuz and Ishtar,* after comparing the Sumerian, Assyrian, and Babylonian calendars and Mesopotamian agricultural cycles, Stephen Langdon concludes:

> This is conclusive evidence that the wailings for Tammuz were held *toward the end of June* from remotest antiquity.[1]

Though the lunar-based calendars of Mesopotamia oscillate with regard to the modern solar-based Gregorian calendar, there are several factors that converge "*toward the end of June.*" Though the festival of Tammuz could begin in early June, the central or median time for its beginning is in the days toward the end of June. Further, the summer solstice, of critical importance on the pagan calendar and linked to the descent of Tammuz, always takes place toward the end of June.

It was no accident that beyond the fact that Pride Month was June, its focus was likewise always the last days of the month, the days "*toward the end of June.*" The commemorations, observances, celebrations, and Pride Parades most often clustered around the days "*toward the end of June.*" They would typically be held within a week or just days from the summer solstice, the time of pagan celebration.

The First Door: Legalization of Homosexuality

At Stonewall the goddess forced open an ancient door. It was the first of several such doors and openings. Among the most momentous of these took place in the United States Supreme Court—in three landmark cases.

The first door and first case was that of *Lawrence v. Texas* in 2003. It resulted in the Supreme Court decision that legalized homosexuality throughout the United States. It would be cited later that same year by the Massachusetts Supreme Court in the ruling that legalized same-sex marriage in that state, the first such legalization in America. *Lawrence v. Texas* represented the opening of the door that had closed on pagan sexuality in ancient times. It was thus covered in the goddess's fingerprints.

When was that Supreme Court decision handed down? It happened in the summer—in *the month of June*. It came *"toward the end of June,"* the specific time that Langdon had cited for the ceremonies and worship of Tammuz and Ishtar. The timing of the Supreme Court decision had nothing to do with the timing of Stonewall any more than the timing of Stonewall had anything to do with the timing of the Reminder Marches. The timing, in this case, was determined by the schedule and functioning of the Supreme Court. And yet every event would converge within days of the others and all at the same time of year ordained for such things in the ancient calendar.

June 26, 2003

More specifically, the ruling that legalized homosexuality across America was handed down on *June 26, 2003*. June 26 was *the same exact date* that the Stonewall uprising was sealed, when its warrant was issued, and the legal authorization was given to set everything else in motion. So the ruling that legalized homosexuality across the nation happened to fall on the anniversary of the day Stonewall was sealed. The mystery had ordained it.

The Second Door: Overturning the Defense of Marriage

The second door was forced open in the landmark Supreme Court case of the *United States v. Windsor* in 2013. It resulted in the ruling that would overturn the Defense of Marriage Act. It would lead to the federal government's recognition of same-sex marriages performed in states where it had, at that point, been legalized. It would also open the door for an even more momentous Supreme Court ruling that would come two years later.

When was the ruling that overturned the Defense of Marriage Act handed down? It happened in the summer of 2013—in *the month of June*—within days of the summer solstice, *"toward the end of June,"* the days especially identified with the festival of Tammuz. It was handed down in the days of the ancient month of Tammuz.

June 26, 2013

On what exact date did the ruling come? The Defense of Marriage Act was overturned on *June 26, 2013—ten years to the exact same day* the Supreme Court legalized homosexuality in 2003. *Both of the rulings* opening the door to the normalization and establishment of homosexuality fell on the same date, and both on the date that sealed Stonewall, the event that began the opening of that door.

The Third Door: The Overturning of Marriage

The third door was forced open in the Supreme Court case of *Obergefell v. Hodges*. It resulted in a momentous ruling that would strike down the historic, biblical, and age-old definition of marriage as the union of a man and woman. It legalized same-sex marriage across America. As marriage was the core relationship of family, and family, the core unit of civilization, the transforming of marriage would ultimately mean the transforming of civilization. The ruling would affect law, education, commerce, religious freedom, and virtually every other realm of American culture. It was monumental, and behind it was the hand of the goddess.

When did it take place? The historical definition of marriage was struck down in the summer—in the month of June, within days of the summer solstice—*toward the end of June*. Marriage as it had always been known was struck down in the ancient month of Tammuz, the month of the goddess's passion.

June 26, 2015

When exactly? Marriage, as the covenant of man and woman, was struck down on *June 26, 2015—the same exact date* that the Defense of Marriage Act was overturned in 2013, *the same exact date* that homosexuality was legalized in 2003, and *the same exact date* that Stonewall was sealed in 1969. And the date that sealed Stonewall was itself the same date on the ancient calendar appointed for the casting of the spell to cause "a man to love a man."[2]

And so all three landmark events that pushed open the ancient door took place on the exact same date. On top of that, each was the anniversary of the date Stonewall was sealed, which was the beginning of the opening of that door—and which was itself, on the ancient calendar, the day appointed for a man to love a man. And thus all four events were joined together and to the ancient day of the ancient spell.

Fingerprints of the Gods

All three Supreme Court rulings took place on one of the days of Tammuz, the ancient month in which the union of male and female was broken. The ninth of Tammuz was the day of the first torchlight procession commemorating the separation of the male and female god. It was on that day that marriage, as the union of male and female, was struck down.

It is hard for the modern mind to fathom the idea that the political, cultural, and judicial events of modern times could be determined by an ancient mystery from the Middle East. But the exact convergence of all these events and factors is stunning.

No one single person was there, present in each of these events, to cause them all to converge. Each series of events was determined by different people, different circumstances, different decisions, different considerations, and different dynamics. One was based on the founding of America; another, on a chaotic uprising that no one could have orchestrated; and another, on the logistics and workings of the Supreme Court. And yet they all fell into place according to the ancient mystery—all three Supreme Court rulings on the exact same day and the day Stonewall was sealed.

They all converged at a time of special import and intensity on the ancient pagan calendar. They all took place at the time specifically connected to an ancient spirit—and the spirit especially connected to the bending of gender and the altering of sexuality.

Night of the Rainbow

On the night that marriage was struck down, a sign appeared across America. It was the sign of the goddess—the rainbow. That night, the sign marked the nation as it never had before.

The sign of the goddess lit up the Empire State Building. It lit up waters of the Niagara Falls. It lit up the iconic castle at Disney World®. And most dramatically, it lit up the building from which America was governed, the White House.

Night of the Ancient Spell

In the ancient Babylonian and Hebrew calendars, each day begins at sundown. The ruling came early in the day that, on the ancient calendar, was the ninth of Tammuz.

But the night that crowned the Supreme Court's overturning of marriage, the night the colors of the rainbow lit up the White House, was a new day on the ancient calendar. It was the tenth of Tammuz. The tenth of Tammuz was the day appointed from ancient times for the spell to be cast to cause "a man to love a man." So the Supreme Court's monumental ruling to overturn marriage, enabling a man to marry a man, was crowned at nightfall by the tenth of Tammuz—the ancient day of the enchantment to cause a man to love a man.

The spell had been cast, and the sign of the goddess marked the land, even the house from which the nation was governed. It was a sign of ownership. The spirit of the goddess was moving to take possession of America.

◆◆◆

To Ishtar belonged the power of metamorphosis by which she could transform a man into a woman and a woman into a man. But what if her powers of metamorphosis were applied to a culture, a nation, or a civilization?

What if the transitioning of a man or woman was a microcosm of the transitioning of an entire culture, nation, and civilization?

Chapter 48

The Grand Metamorphosis

To CHANGE A man into a woman or a woman into a man is to change identity. Thus the goddess possessed the power to transform identity. So she would now set out to transform the identity of America. The American metamorphosis that spanned the mid-twentieth century to the early twenty-first century was so radical and profound that the latter America would be largely unrecognizable to the former.

The Altering of Memory

One's identity is rooted in one's past. So to completely transform another's identity, one would have to alter their past or their memory of it, or how they perceived it. So the spirit of the goddess would set out to alter America's memory. It would have to be rewritten. America would be given an altered memory, an altered history. Old landmarks and monuments would be reinterpreted or removed. New landmarks and new monuments would be established. The Stonewall Inn, the site of the uprising against the police, would now become a national landmark.

A new history, a new national memory, would be inculcated into the minds of American children in classrooms across the country. And as time went on and the metamorphosis progressed, the nation was less and less able to remember what it had once been or that it had ever been anything other than what it now was. A transitioned past would produce a transitioned nation and a transitioned future.

The Transitioning of America

To transform a man into a woman or a woman into a man means the transforming of priorities, proclivities, values, and desires. The man who desired women and not men would now, as a woman, presumably desire men and not women. Each would now accept what they had once rejected and reject what they had once accepted.

So it would be in the goddess's transitioning of America. She would change the nation's priorities, proclivities, values, and desires. What the culture once rejected, it would now accept; and what it once accepted, it would now reject. What it once saw as wrong, immoral, or evil, it would

209

now see as good, and what it once saw as good, it would now see as wrong, immoral, or evil. What it once found abhorrent or shocking, it now venerated as sacred, and what it once venerated as sacred, it now found abhorrent and shocking. As the spirit of the goddess transitioned male to female and female to male, it was now transitioning a Christian civilization; it was being altered, step-by-step, into a pagan one, and "one nation under God" into "one nation under the gods."

Becoming the Opposite

For the goddess to change a man into a woman or a woman into a man, she had to nullify the original nature and biological state into which the individual was born. So to transition America, she would cause the nation to war against its own foundation, its original nature, and its historic identity. She would cause the nation to hate and condemn what it once was. She would do likewise to Western civilization. Both America and Western civilization would be transitioned into the opposite of what they had been.

Accompanying the transformation was her sign—the rainbow. It became the ubiquitous sign of the transformation. She had used her ancient strategy and her mode of battle and retaliation. She *stretched herself like a rainbow across the sky* and reached thereby as far as the earth.[1] So it was again through the sign of the rainbow that the goddess was able to *stretch* herself across the landscape of American culture and the modern world and enlarge herself and her movement.

Every year it seemed as if the rainbow grew in presence and power. It was a sign that the goddess's power was likewise growing. The symbol from the fringe of American culture was now taking it over. The sign of the goddess began appearing everywhere, in stores, on mugs, on T-shirts, on blankets, on stationery, and on merchandise of every kind.

Crosses Into Rainbows

In ancient times the goddess was linked to government and political power. So she would be again. The American government would come under her spell. While crosses and other symbols representing God, Scripture, and the Christian faith were being removed from public property and the public square, the sign of the goddess was brought in to be displayed in their place. The rainbow was enshrined in the public square. It began manifesting on public property, in municipal halls, and in government buildings.

So too law enforcement would begin coming under her spell. Police officers would now march in her processions. And the rainbow now began appearing on police cars. The Stonewall uprising had begun as a war against the police. Now the goddess was beginning to take them over.

Emblems and Logos

The American flag represented the nation to the world. It was flown outside every American embassy in every nation where there was an American embassy. But a new banner was now being flown along with the American flag on American embassies—the rainbow flag. It was unprecedented. The sign of the goddess now became, in effect, a representation of America. It was a sign that America itself was now being transitioned.

So too the corporate world would become subject to the goddess's spirit. Major corporations now began not only adopting her agenda but sanctifying her sign. They created new versions of their own logos rendered in the colors of the rainbow.

During Pride Month, they would proudly display their rainbow logos to the world. Logos represent identity. The new altered rainbow logos were a sign. The goddess was altering their logos as she was altering their identities. She was transitioning them as well.

Children of the Rainbow

The goddess and her fellow gods were especially interested in children. If she could transition them, if she could change their nature, she could alter the future. She could possess the world. So the sign of the goddess began appearing on the flagpoles in front of their schools—high schools, middle schools, and then elementary schools. In classrooms across America, children were now being taught to revere the rainbow flag, to hallow the rainbow flag, and to follow the ways of the goddess.

And when the children came home from school, they would see her sign appearing in their cartoons on television and in their games, videos, and postings on the internet, likewise inducting them to her service. Even the packaging on children's snacks, cookies, and candies would now bear the sign of the goddess. Even cereal boxes were now covered in rainbows and words that urged the children to embrace sexual identities other than what they had been born into. The nation's children were being placed in the goddess's hands.

En Toutoi Nika

The ascendancy of the rainbow and all that it stood for was not a natural phenomenon. It was supernatural. Its veneration was not based on logic—but on a spirit, the spirit of a goddess. It was the sign of her presence, her power, and her dominion. Everywhere the image appeared, everywhere the rainbow flag was raised, her powers increased. She had begun with a handful of followers at Stonewall. Now she had placed her mark of ownership on countless millions and on America itself.

The conversion of the Roman emperor Constantine was one of the most important events in world history. It happened through a sign. Before his battle against the emperor Maxentius at the Milvian Bridge in AD 312, Constantine saw a vision. Above the sun was a cross of light and the Greek words *en toutoi nika*, "In this, conquer." The sign was thus crucial in the conversion of a pagan civilization into a Christian one.

But now there was another sign—the rainbow. And by that sign the goddess would war against the cross. In that sign she would also set out to conquer. The rainbow was likewise a sign of conversion—but this time the conversion would be of a Christian civilization into a pagan one.

So the appearance of the rainbow was, in and of itself, a sign that a once Christian nation and a once Christian civilization were in metamorphosis to paganism. The goddess's hands were at work, performing a surgery of spirit. They were all being transitioned.

———◆◆◆———

As we approach the last section, we will focus on the end of things, the end of the mystery, the endgame of the gods, the last of all states, and the conclusions we must draw. And we will ask and answer the final questions:

Why have the gods returned?

What is their aim?

What lies ahead?

And what does it have to do with each of us, now, in the days to come, and beyond?

Part X:

WAR OF

THE GODS

Chapter 49

Vengeance of the Gods

WE MUST NOW ask the question: If the gods that were cast out with the coming of Christianity returned, would they not come back with a vengeance—and would not their vengeance be focused on those who cast them out?

If the birth of the Christian faith meant the end of the gods, then upon their return, would they not seek its end?

The Two-Thousand-Year-Old Vendetta

As the gods had thrived in a *pre*-Christian age, they would now seek to usher in a *post*-Christian age.

And if the entrance of Christianity brought about the casting out of the gods from Western civilization, then upon their reentering, they would seek to bring about the casting out of Christianity from Western civilization.

Or in the context of the parable, as the spirits had been cast out of the house, they could only return by casting out that by which they had themselves been cast out, the Spirit of God. The spirits would wage war against that which had waged war against them, the Spirit of God, the Word of God, the ways of God, the house of God, and the people of God.

Into the Catacombs

As the gods had been driven out of the mainstream of culture of the ancient world, they would now seek to drive God and those who followed Him out of the mainstream of modern culture. As the gods had once been driven to the margins and shadows of their culture, they would now seek to drive Christians to the margins, to the shadows, to the closets and catacombs of modern culture.

Silencing of the Word

The gods had once been silenced by the Word of God. So now they would seek to silence the Word of God and the Christians who upheld it. They would work to drive the Word out of Western culture just as the Word had once driven them out. The gods had seen laws enacted against them, encroaching on their worship and temples. So now they would work to have laws enacted in Western nations that would encroach upon Christianity, its worship, churches, and ministries.

Children of the Gods

It was ultimately the young who undid the gods. The children of the late Roman Empire were no longer effectively indoctrinated into paganism. They were now taught of the new faith and against the rites and worship of the gods.

So upon their return, the gods would seek to undo their undoing. The removal of prayer and Scripture was only the beginning. They would seek to gain control of the young. And they would do so through the media, through television, through the internet, and through the classroom.

The children would increasingly be taught to reject Christianity and despise biblical values. With or without the mention of the gods, they would be indoctrinated into their ways, into pagan values, so that the ways of God would become alien to them.

At the same time, the gods would attack the transmission of the Christian faith from parent to child and from teacher to student in Christian schools and universities. As they had once been cut off from influencing the young and cast out by a new generation, the gods would now seek to cut off the young from the Christian faith and to use the new generation to cast out the Christian faith and bring Judeo-Christian civilization to an end.

The Dark Trinity's War

It was war. And the gods of the dark trinity were ready for battle. Baal was a warrior. Molech was a murderer. And as for Ishtar, she was both a warrior and the executor of vengeance. And it would be her sword that would serve as the most prominent weapon in the war to destroy the faith that had cast her out. As the goddess of sexuality, gender-crossing, and battle, she would employ all three in a massive and multifront campaign of annihilation against Christians and their faith.

When the historic and biblical definition of marriage was struck down in June of 2015, many saw it as a watermark not only in the history of America but of Western civilization. Age-old biblical standards and values concerning sexuality, marriage, and gender were discarded and replaced overnight with pagan ones. Christians were now told that they would have to comply with the new morality, its tenets and acts, to endorse them and propagate them, by force of social or economic pressure or by force of law. If they refused or voiced disagreement, they would now be subject to serious consequences: the loss of their jobs, the boycotting of their businesses, deplatforming, defunding, prosecution, or other punishments.

There was now a new phenomenon that had no precedent in the West—the placing of Christians on trial in once Christian nations for the crime of quoting the Bible. Such trials almost always concerned sexuality and gender, the issues and workings of the goddess.

She Cuts to Pieces Him

It was not new to the gods. Before they departed Western civilization, they had waged war against the new faith and the first Christians. They were able at first to depict them as different, alien, foreigners, and a danger to society. They incited the people to fear and hate them. They moved upon the ancient magistrates and mobs to war against them, silence them, imprison them, and brutally murder them for public sport.

One of the gods that warred against the first believers was Venus. Venus was Ishtar. So it was written in one of her ancient Mesopotamian hymns:

She cuts to pieces him who shows no respect.[1]

In the war that was waged in ancient times against the gospel, the gods would cause Christians to be literally cut to pieces.

But as more and more people embraced the new faith, the gods could no longer depict Christians as alien, as different, or as a danger to society. And when the gods were finally sent into exile, the persecution of Christians came to a decisive end.

The Great Persecution: Part 2

For most of the following centuries, the gods and spirits were in no position to wage war or incite a persecution against those who upheld the Scriptures or followed Jesus. They were hiding in the shadows. And in the early days of their return to the modern world, their position was too marginal and weak to launch any kind of persecution.

But it was only a matter of time before that would change. As soon as they had become established, they would begin working toward the marginalization, encroachment, and persecution of believers.

As the West began de-Christianizing and re-paganizing, the gods could again begin depicting Christians as different, alien, foreign, and a danger to society. Again they could begin setting the culture to war against them. Again they could incite a generation to fear and hate them. And now the gods had powers unavailable to them in ancient times—mass media, social media, the worldwide web. And as in the days of Rome, they could portray Christian dissent from sin as intolerance and hate-mongering and the speaking of God's Word as a blasphemy, an act of criminality.

In an earlier day the values upheld by Christians would have been lauded as virtues. But now they would be despised. The Christians had not changed, but the culture around them had. It had been transformed so totally that it could not even remember ever being otherwise—that it had once been Christian. So for the first time in two thousand years, believers found themselves in the midst of a pagan civilization. And just as it had two thousand years earlier, it would mean persecution.

Against the Throne of God

The gods had an ancient score to settle with their enemies. They would now make up for lost time. They were dangerous. The danger they posed could not be measured by anything seen thus far, for it was tied to how much power they possessed. And their power was continually increasing—so too the danger.

In the myth of the gardener, the goddess stretched herself across the sky like a rainbow for the purpose of executing vengeance. The rainbow would again be linked to vengeance. But this time it would be directed against believers. Behind its colors were centuries of pent-up fury.

It was, as well, a sign of war against God. It was always the goddess's nature to take what belonged to others and use them for herself. The rainbow belonged to God. It is described in Scripture as being part of the glory that surrounds His throne. It was also the sign of His mercy in the wake of judgment. But the goddess of transformation had transformed the sign of God into a sign of defiance against the ways of God—it was a banner of war. Those who joined in its display had no idea what they were doing or that they were being drawn into an ancient war against the throne of God.

◆◆◆

The gods had been expelled, and they had now returned. They would seek retribution against those who had cast them out and sent them into exile. In ancient times, their fury was so fierce that it caused the Christians to be led into the arenas to be devoured by wild animals to the cheers of the Roman masses. To what would it lead now?

———◆◆◆———

Could the growing movement to curtain free speech in the West, whether in the form of political correctness, wokeism, cancel culture, or the growing danger of *soft totalitarianism*, be connected to the mystery of the gods?

And could the day come, as it came in ancient times, when the refusal to bow one's knee before the gods would incur the most grave of consequences?

Chapter 50

Every Knee Shall Bow

THE GODS HAD come back not only to exact vengeance but for dominion. They had returned to reign.

In ancient times they had reigned over the cultures in which they were enshrined. But when those cultures turned to God, they were forced to abdicate, to leave their thrones and go into exile. Having returned, they would again lift their scepters and aspire to mastery and dominion.

Kingship of the Gods

Baal, the first of the dark trinity, was known as "King of the gods" and "Lord of the earth." The name "Baal"—or "Lord," "Owner," and "Master"—was not only his title but a description of his nature. He would seek to master, to own, and to lord. In his mythologies, he battled other Canaanite gods to gain or regain lordship and authority. The ancient "Baal Epic" reveals his ambition:

> Mighty Baal…desired the kingship of the Gods.[1]

And he would have it. He would become the undisputed lord of the Canaanite deities.

The same spirit would war against the God of Israel.

The Days of Baal

It was through a spirit of tolerance and openness that Baal gained entrance into the culture of ancient Israel.

But once his worship and cult became widespread and established, once it touched the highest levels of authority, everything changed. The tolerance of earlier days came to an end. It had served its function as a doorway through which Baal could enter. Baal now reigned as the nation's god, and there would be no room for the nation's former God. He would seek to achieve total domination. Everyone would now be required to call him "Baal," or "Lord."

Anyone and anything that now stood in his way was to be eliminated. He would war against God and His people and anyone who still upheld the former ways. He would use all means at His disposal, the power of culture, the power of state, and the power of his cult. Those who held to and upheld the ways of God would now be branded as troublemakers, agitators, and enemies of the state. Thus came the days when the righteous were persecuted and the prophets were hunted down—the days of Baal.

The Opening and the Closing

It goes back to the ancient parable. The spirits seek to return to the house.

When one is trying to get into a house, one seeks openness. One pushes to open its door. So when the gods were seeking to get into the American house and that of Western civilization, the focus was on *openness* and *tolerance*. It was never really about either. *Openness* and *tolerance* were only the means of opening the door and to gain entrance. They were the way to cause a nation and a civilization to abandon the values they had long cherished for what was new and foreign. It was for that reason that the entrance of the gods was most dramatically seen in the 1960s, when *openness* and *tolerance* were sacred mantras.

But once one gets through the door and inside the house, one no longer seeks openness. If one's aim is to stay in the house, then one now seeks to close the door. So once the gods came into America and became established, once people started accepting their ways and authorities, the ideal of openness would now work against them.

They had to consolidate their power. They had to close the door. So there was a change in the atmosphere. A chill came over free speech. The doors began to close. Any dissent from the new morality could now be met with punishment. One was free to endorse the new ways of the gods, but one was not free to challenge them.

Most people had no idea why it was happening or how it could change so dramatically. But it was the logical conclusion to the entrance of the gods.

Baals of the Universe

So as it was in the days of Baal in ancient Israel, it was in America. The earlier tolerance would be replaced by a new "enlightened" intolerance. It would manifest as *political correctness,* then *wokeness,* and *cancel culture.* Every word that could now be interpreted as expressing dissent from the newly sanctioned view was subject to judgment and censure. Anything that could be interpreted as challenging or differing from the new morality had to be canceled.

In ancient Israel, Baal could use kings and queens, an Ahab and a

Jezebel, as his vessels to stamp out dissent and cancel the opposition. But now, in addition to the powers of state, Baal could employ technology, social media, the internet to stamp out dissent and cancel the opposition. And with more and more communication taking place online, Baal and his fellow gods could control human speech, behavior, and thought in a way that was never before possible.

It was no accident that in the last days before the destruction of Jerusalem, the prophet Jeremiah was thrown into prison. The gods had taken over the culture and, through the nation's leaders, had sought to silence the prophets and all opposition. The tolerance for new gods had now morphed into a culture of oppression—a cancel culture.

In the modern case the leaders of Silicon Valley were more than willing to comply with the new directives of Baal. That which challenged the authority of the new gods would, at their hands, be canceled. Baal had been heralded as "*Lord of the Earth.*" The leaders of Big Tech had been labeled the "*Masters of the Universe.*" In biblical Hebrew, the word *master* is Baal. So the title could be rendered the "*Baals of the Universe.*"

Ishtar Unleashed

But Baal was not the only god seeking dominion. As the name *Baal* means *lord,* the name *Molech* means *king.* Molech would seek his own kingdom. He could use the abortion industry and the extreme and the radically woke as his instruments.

Then there was Ishtar. She too sought dominion. She craved it, even if it meant taking over the dominions of other gods. She took the powers of civilization away from her father. She attempted to take control of the underworld from her sister. And she was believed to have taken over the Eanna temple from the sky god, An.

Ishtar would accept nothing less than the total submission of her subjects. If they refused, she would respond with fury. In one of her myths, she rages against a mountain that failed to show her reverence:

> As I, the goddess, approached the mountain it showed me no respect….Since they showed me no respect, since they did not put their noses to the ground for me, since they did not rub their lips in the dust for me, I shall personally fill the soaring mountain range with my terror.[2]

Since Ishtar was the goddess of war, her response to any perceived lack of homage or submission could be especially calamitous and deadly. She would seek to destroy any who did not reverence her.

Her return to the modern world came, as it did for the other gods, through the doorway of tolerance. And upon gaining power, her focus would turn to dominion. Anyone who refused to pay her homage, anyone refusing to go along with her altering of sexuality, marriage, and gender, would suffer the unleashing of her fury. She would vilify them, portray them as haters, incite the culture against them, and seek to deprive them of their livelihood, their speech, and their freedom.

The Totalitarian Gods

It was a strange transformation. Cultures that had for so long espoused the virtues of freedom and tolerance would suddenly begin espousing the virtues of intolerance. Nations that had long venerated free speech as a sacred pillar of their democracy now venerated its suppression. But it was all part of the mystery ushered in by the returning gods.

The "open" culture that welcomed them in began closing up. In place of tolerance and freedom of speech came ideological conformity and the crushing of speech and thought. They were signs. The gods were consolidating their hold on America and Western culture.

One now had to watch every word that came out of one's mouth, every comment one posted online, even one's own thoughts. If one spoke or wrote in a way that violated the new dogmas of the gods, they were to be punished or were forced to publicly confess their sins. It was a new totalitarianism, birthed of the gods' new dominion.

The fury of the new order would fall on those who resisted it. It would fall, first of all, on those who upheld the ways of God, the Christians, those who followed God's Word. Conservatives would also be targeted. The reason was simple: conservatives sought to conserve; the gods sought to overturn.

But even liberals who were not radical enough now found themselves under siege by the more radical new guard. Liberal professors now found themselves attacked by their students for upholding free speech and in danger of losing their jobs. Old school feminists now came under fire for upholding the existence of women against the campaign to abolish them.

But they had all been used of the gods. And now the agenda was moving to another stage and passing them by. They could be disposed of. The revolution the gods had inaugurated was devouring its own children.

Every Knee Shall Bow

And though it was now dressed in modern clothing, the phenomenon was as old as Baal. When he had gained dominion in Israel, every knee was to bow before him. Those who refused to bow were risking death. So too in Babylon, the Jewish peers of the prophet Daniel were commanded to bow down to a golden idol. They would not and so would be sentenced to execution. In Rome the Christians were compelled to worship the gods of Rome. Those who refused did so at risk of imprisonment and execution.

In each case, the persecution was connected to the gods and to the act of bowing down. It had always been their nature to force every knee to bow down in their presence. It was this that lay behind the new totalitarianism. In their newfound dominion, the gods moved upon government and corporate organizations to force their employees to attend indoctrination sessions into the ways of wokeness and the new codes of ethics, expelled students from schools and universities for affirming the existence of male and female, forced parents to transition their children, brought lawsuits against shopkeepers for refusing to violate their faith, and compelled others to give homage to the sign of the rainbow.

Many were mystified by the transformation overtaking their culture. But the phenomenon was ancient. The gods were doing as they had done in ancient times. They would not rest until every knee had bowed down before them and every tongue confessed that they were the new and undisputed lords.

Dominion

The gods had promised that, in exchange for abandoning God, they would usher in a culture of freedom. But instead they had ushered in a culture in which every knee, word, and thought was forced to bow down in their veneration.

Nations whose core identities were based on freedom and opposition to totalitarianism now discarded the first and freely adopted the latter. Having turned away from God, they found themselves compelled to kneel before their new masters.

The spirits now inhabited government chambers, corporate boardrooms, college campuses, courtrooms, television, movie and computer screens, music, popular culture, youth culture, children's culture, and virtually every corner of American and Western society. The new totalitarianism was a sign that the gods had achieved their dominion. They had successfully transformed a Christian civilization into a pagan one.

And as for those who had defied their dominion and would not bow their knee, the gods would pass the same judgment on them as they had on those who resisted them in ancient times—there would be no room for them in the dominion of the gods.

What is the end of the mystery? To where does it all lead?

The answer was there from the beginning, in the valleys, in the groves, in their temples, and on the high places. The answer lay on the altars.

Chapter 51

Altars of the Gods

THE PROPHET WALKED through the ruins of the holy city and wept. He had foretold its destruction. He had warned the people against the gods. But they rejected the warning. They continued in their course, turning all the more from God and all the more to their gods and idols. The gods had promised to give them prosperity, freedom, and fulfillment. But they had now given them their gift—destruction. Jerusalem now lay in ruins and burning ash, and the nation was no more.

The Altars

It was the inevitable conclusion. It was the nature of the gods to bring destruction. Their worship involved altars. Their altars involved blood—even the blood of children. That was the price of following them. That was the demand of the spirits.

It is no accident that those most closely joined to the gods were those most likely to engage in acts of self-destruction. The priests of Baal slashed themselves. The priests of Ishtar spilled their own blood in the goddess's processions. And the worshippers of Molech offered up as blood sacrifices their own flesh and blood in the form of their children.

The gods destroyed their own. The gods caused them to destroy themselves and to celebrate their own destruction.

The Keys of Destruction

How did they do it? How did they cause their followers to destroy themselves? They removed from the lives of their subjects purpose and meaning. When life has no meaning, no purpose, no absolute value, it then proceeds toward death and destruction. The lives of children can then be disposed of and sacrificed. If the gods can remove purpose from sexuality, it can be repurposed in any direction, and it will stop producing life. Then it will give birth instead to death. If the gods can remove man from manhood and woman from womanhood, it will bring about destruction, the disintegration of family, society, and lives. If they can remove the purpose of marriage, then it too will disintegrate. When purpose is removed, destruction follows.

So they did to ancient Israel. They drew the nation of God away from God and from the purpose for which it had been created. The gods removed the nation's reason for existing. And it ceased to exist.

Filling the Altar

So when the gods returned to the modern world, they set out to do the same. Sexuality was again removed from marriage, man from manhood, woman from womanhood, marriage from the state of marriage, humanity from humanity, and life from life. Behind it all was the removal of purpose. From that would come destruction. And in destruction their altars would be filled.

The purpose of life can only be found in the One who created it—God. Therefore, to be separated from God is to be separated from one's purpose and reason for existing. And so the returning gods set their focus on separating all from God and each from its purpose.

Judgment Time

As the day of Israel's destruction neared, the shadow of the gods deepened. It was then that the prophet Jeremiah stood overlooking the valley where the Israelites had built altars to Baal and Molech and sacrificed their children. It was then that he prophesied the nation's destruction and smashed the potter's jar on the ground.

It was then that the prophet Ezekiel was taken in a vision into the Temple courts and saw the women of Israel, in the spirit of Ishtar, weeping for Tammuz. It was then that he saw the elders of Israel in the Temple's inner courts worshipping the sun. And it was then that he heard the command given for the judgment to begin.

The nation's judgment was bound to the gods. The nation's destruction would come from Babylon and Mesopotamia, the land of the goddess and her fellow gods. Those who carried out the destruction were the worshippers and servants of the Babylonian and Mesopotamian gods.

It would all begin in the month dedicated to the goddess and her lover, the month of Tammuz, the time of the summer festival, the "*June parades.*" It was on the ninth day of Tammuz when the soldiers of Babylon broke through the defensive walls of Jerusalem. The city's hedge of protection was removed. Destruction would now be only a matter of time. The ninth of Tammuz would be commemorated as a national day of sorrow and mourning.

Centuries later the walls of Jerusalem would again be breached, this time by another pagan army, that of Rome. The judgment would begin in the same month—Tammuz. The Roman breaching of the city on the seventeenth day of that month would, as well, be commemorated as a national day of sorrow and mourning.

In each case, the destruction began in the same month, the month of the god linked to Ishtar. That the nation's judgment began in Tammuz was significant as well since Tammuz was the month of the nation's apostasy and judgment, starting with the golden calf. So the judgment came in the days of the gods. It was fitting, as it was the gods to which the nation had turned that would bring about its destruction.

Warning of Judgment

What about America? The gods brought judgment and destruction to Israel. Could America likewise be in danger of judgment and destruction? Both nations had been dedicated to God at their inception, both had turned away from God, both had followed the gods Baal, Molech, and the goddess.

But America had gone further. It had become the world's primary vessel for the return of the gods. It had become the world's chief proponent of materialism, the worship of prosperity, and money, sexual immorality, pornography, abortion, homosexuality, transsexuality, and the alteration of gender. America had singlehandedly resurrected the goddess's midsummer festivals and processions, which now covered the world.

America had hallowed and championed the sign of the rainbow, not only within its borders, but around the world. To take the sign given of God's mercy in the wake of judgment and turn it against the ways of God is to call upon oneself a judgment with no mercy.

So too America had chosen to strike down the ways of God in the month of the goddess and her lover, the month of gods and judgment. And it was no accident that it struck down the biblical hedge of marriage on the ninth of Tammuz, the very day that Israel's protective hedge was struck down, and that opened the way for the nation's judgment.

The prophets warned Israel that to turn away from God to follow after the gods would lead to destruction. America has turned away from God and now follows after the gods. To what then will it lead? It must as well, in the end, lead to destruction.

But judgment applies not only to nations—but to people. It applies to each of us. To partake in a nation's war against God, to join in its defiance of

God, to celebrate the destruction of His ways, to lead little children into confusion and alter their physical beings and thus to cause, in the words of Jesus, these *"little ones to stumble,"* to cause these still more little ones to be killed, or to passively condone such things by doing and saying nothing to stop them, is to partake in judgment and to invoke judgment upon one's own life.

Then what are we to do?

Is there an answer to the gods and judgment?

Is there hope?

For that we must go further. We must bring all things to their conclusion. And we must take one more step beyond the gods—to another.

Chapter 52

The Other God

S o WHAT DOES the return of the gods tell us?

It tells us that there is more to human events, to world history, and even to our own lives, more than we can imagine. Behind the natural realm lies a more than natural realm. And that which is more than natural can be good or evil. We are largely unaware of how the other realm is affecting our world and lives. But at times it manifests so strongly that it becomes hard to rationalize or ignore.

Nazi Germany is one such case. It is so extreme that any attempt to explain it without accounting for that which is beyond the natural is destined to fail. It was not of the natural but of a realm that is more than natural. And what is now happening to America and Western civilization is no less beyond the natural and of the other realm.

A Most Dangerous Thing

The mystery also tells us, as in the house of spirits, that for a nation or civilization that has known God and turned away from Him and, more specifically, that has known the gospel and turned away from it—it is a most dangerous thing.

And it is this that lies behind the strange and disturbing transformations overtaking American culture and Western civilization—the rise of irrational ideologies; the nullifying of biology; the denial of reality; the emergence of quasi-religious "secular" movements; the deterioration and transmutation of marriage, family, and gender; the alteration of children; the abolition of man and woman; the murder of the most innocent; the disintegration of society as we have known it; the rise of a new and subtle totalitarianism; and the silencing of all that question such things.

Even many secular observers and those of no faith have noted that it seems as if something has come to possess American and Western culture; something has taken it over. But we should not be surprised at what is happening. The mystery ordains it. A house that has emptied itself of God cannot remain empty. It will be seized and taken over by that which is not God. And when a civilization expels God from its midst, it never ends well.

What we are now witnessing is as momentous as the Christianization of Western civilization at the beginning of this age—only it is its opposite. It is the casting out of the spirits in reverse. It is their invoking, their conjuring, and their reentrance. It is the repossession of the house. And according to the parable, when the spirits repossess the house, its last state will be worse than its first.

The Great Apostasy

It is a basic tendency of human nature not to realize what one has until one no longer has it. Rarely do we discern the danger from which we are being protected until the protection is removed. When light is removed, its absence will always be occupied by darkness. And when God is removed, His absence will be occupied by evil.

So the Bible foretells that in the last days there will be a great falling away from the faith, a great apostasy. It is now taking place. It also foretells that in the last days evil and immorality will increase and persecution will come for Christians, for all who hold true to the ways of God.

The parable warns that the last state will be worse than the first, and the last state is not yet finished. We can therefore expect the dark to grow darker still. We have thus not yet seen the last or the worst of the gods.

Against the Gods

How then is one to live in the days when the civilization around us has become a house of spirits? How can one stand against the darkness of the house, resist its intimidations, refuse its temptations, defy its powers? How can one stand against the gods?

One cannot stand against the gods and be serving them at the same time. We must remember—that which we most serve, most dwell upon, most rejoice in, and most live for; that which most moves us, draws us, impels us; that which is our greatest joy and ultimate end—that is our god. And if we serve any of the gods, we cannot stand against them.

We must renounce any and all gods and any hold they have on our lives. Though in their house, we must be not *of* their house. We must take no part in their ways, have no communion with their spirits, leave no gap for their entrance, and pay no heed to their commandments.

If the age is ruled by the gods, and our culture by the spirits, if its leaders are led by them, and the majority are impelled by them, then how does one stand? By what power? Only a power strong enough to resist them. And there is only one. There is only one antidote.

The Elohim Mystery

The only answer to the gods—is God. The powers of the gods can only be overcome by the power of God. In the Hebrew Scriptures the word for God is *Elohim*. *Elohim* is plural. It speaks of the one true God in His transcendence and limitlessness. But the same word, translated as *"God,"* is, in other contexts, translated as *"the gods."* The strange property of the word reveals a profound truth. In the end, it will come down to one *Elohim* or the other—the *Elohim* of God or the *elohim* of the gods.

We were each created with an emptiness that can only be filled by God's presence. Our hearts possess a God-shaped vacuum. So no matter what else we have, without God our lives and hearts remain empty. But if we are not filled by Elohim, by God, we will end up being filled by the elohim—by the gods. The elohim of the gods manifests in many forms and appearances. Whether it is the elohim of money, success, pleasure, acceptance, self-obsession, addiction, or any other thing, they are, in the end, elohim, substitutes for the absence of the One who is Elohim, God.

We were each made to seek and find Him. But if we do not find the Elohim of God, we will end up serving and worshipping the elohim of the gods. The pagan world was filled with them. But the center of that world was empty, darkened, restless, without peace, purpose, or hope. So the apostle Paul described the condition of those living in paganism as

> …having no hope and without God in the world.[1]

Modern culture, having turned away from God and to the gods, is now marked by the same signs that once marked the ancient pagan world: purposelessness, emptiness, and hopelessness. And the answer to the modern world is the same as to the ancient, and all the more so—God.

No One Among the Gods

The answer is even more specific. When the pagan world was set free from its bondage to the gods, it was set free through a specific name, the name of *Yeshua*, Jesus. The name stood out among the gods. In Hebrew it means *"The Lord is salvation."* For the pagan world it meant that there was one God and only one who could actually bring freedom and bring redemption.

Yeshua, Jesus, was unique among the gods in every way. He did not exist in a mythological world of fantasy and imagination but in real time and real space, in the flesh-and-blood realm of historical reality. He did not walk the mythical regions of the underworld, the fields of Elysium or the halls of Valhalla, but the dry and dusty roads of first-century Judea. The gospel message of His death and resurrection was not based on a recurring mythological cycle but on the historical accounting of those who witnessed it and who neither expected it to happen nor understood it when it did—but whose lives were then radically transformed by it.

In his song of praise to God, Moses asked, "Who is like You, O Lord, among the gods?"[2] There had never been one among the gods like Yeshua, Jesus of Nazareth. There had never been one among the gods with a message so wholly centered on so radical a love. There had never been one among the gods who told His followers that they were to love even their enemies and forgive those who persecuted them.

There had never been one among the gods who was called the *"Friend of Sinners,"* nor one who had so loved and reached out to the outcast, the rejected, the broken, and the lost. There had never been one among the gods who could say to the world, *"I am the way, the truth, and the life,"*[3] and, *"Come to Me, all you who are weary and burdened, and I will give you rest,"*[4] and have such words ring true. Nor had there ever been one among the gods who not only spoke of so radical a love but who actually lived and died as its embodiment.

The Other Altar

Where there were gods, there were altars. The gods demanded sacrifices, even if the sacrifices were the children of their worshippers. Yeshua also had an altar. But there were none among the altars of the gods like His altar. Nor had any god done what He had done. Instead of demanding that He be given a sacrifice, He alone gave His life as the sacrifice. Instead of taking life, He *gave* His life—so that life would be given to the world, to all who would receive it.

On the first Passover, it is written that the gods of Egypt were brought into judgment and the people of God were set free from their bondage. It is no accident that the day on which Jesus died was Passover. For it is by that that the powers and strongholds of the gods are broken. And by that, those who were enslaved and under their bondage are set free.

He was the opposite of the gods. He was their antidote. To Him belonged the power to cast out the spirits and set free the possessed. It is no accident that it was He who cast out the gods of the pagan world and set free an empire and a civilization that had been possessed and ruled of them.

The Antidote to the Gods

The uniqueness of Yeshua, Jesus, was not confined to the ancient world. His influence and impact on the world would exceed and outlast that of every other leader, ruler, power, nation, and empire. He would become the central figure of our planet. Every moment of human history, every event that took place on earth, would be marked and dated by its relation to His birth.

Even two thousand years after His coming, even in the modern world, there was still none like Him among the gods. There was none so feared and hated by them. He had cast them out of the ancient world, and upon their return, they would wage war against Him, against His Word and people. And so the persecution against Christians would be greater in the modern world than it had been in the ancient world, greater than in the days of the Roman arenas.

But that fact revealed a critical truth: He was, in the modern world, as much as He had been in the ancient, the only antidote to the gods—the only answer. As it was in the ancient world, so too in the modern—in Him alone was the power to break their chains, pull down their strongholds, nullify their spells and curses, and set their captives free.

The Infinite Answer

As the presence of darkness is dependent on the absence of light, so the power of the gods was and is dependent on the absence of God. It was that absence in the ancient pagan world that allowed them to rule and thrive. And it was that same absence in the apostasy of the modern world that allowed the gods to return.

So in order to achieve dominion, the gods had to separate nations, cultures, and civilizations from God—and also individuals. If one is separated from God, one is subject to the gods, to the powers of darkness.

But the power of Yeshua, Jesus, is the opposite. It is the power to end the separation, to remove everything that has separated us from God, starting with sin—as all have sinned. And a single sin is enough to create an infinite separation from the One who is infinitely good. And an infinite separation requires an infinite answer to bridge the gap. And so only an infinite life and an infinite love, the life and love of God given in Yeshua, in sacrifice on the cross, can fill the gap, end the separation, and bring reconciliation and redemption.

And so the gospel message that came into the pagan world was this: by the death of Jesus of Nazareth, there is forgiveness for sin—every sin, redemption for every life, and the ending of every separation from God. And by His resurrection from death, there is restoration of all brokenness, the nullifying of every curse, and eternal life—for all who will receive it.

Gehenna and Heaven

The generation of Israelites that followed the gods perished in judgment while sacrificing their children in the Valley of Hinnom. In Hebrew, the Valley of Hinnom was called *Gei Hinnom*. The name would become *Gehenna*. *Gehenna* is another name for hell. The gods had led them there. The gods lead to hell. They are bent on death and destruction. They are the spirits of hell.

But the other God is bent on heaven and eternal life. The message of salvation is that Yeshua, Jesus, bore your judgment so that you would never have to. And by that salvation, you are set free from all darkness, all sin, all judgment, and all hell and given life, here and now and forever—heaven. It is the power to nullify the past, to end the old life, and to begin anew, to be born of God, born of heaven, born again.

The True God and How to Receive Him

There is no life so far from God that His mercy cannot reach it. There is no sin one has committed that is so great that His forgiveness is not greater still; no bondage, no addiction, no chain so strong that it can withstand His power to break it; no past so defiled, so full of guilt and shame, that His power to redeem it is not still greater; and no darkness so dark that His love is not deeper still. He is the light that drives out all darkness, the hope that overcomes all hopelessness, the grace that washes away all sin, guilt, and shame, and the way that breaks open every wall and barrier and makes possible what was not. His arms are still open, and His love is calling. One only has to say yes to receive it, to receive Him.

How? It is as simple as opening one's heart and life to the love of God, to give Him one's sins and burdens, one's all, to receive Him into one's life, to let His presence come into one's heart, His light into the darkness, His forgiveness, His cleansing, His Word, His peace, His Spirit into every part of one's life, to turn away from all darkness, all sin, all idols, and all gods, to put one's faith in Yeshua, Jesus, as one's Lord and Savior, and to begin following Him as His disciple all the days of one's life.

It is as simple as making Him who is the only Lord the true Lord of your life, and Him who is the only true God the true God of your life.

Overcoming the World

And so we return to the question: How then is one to live in a civilization that has become a house of spirits?

The only way is by the power of God. It is only by His power that one can stand against the gods. It is only by His love that one can overcome all hatred. Only by His grace can one overcome all sin. Only by His hand can one break the chains of all bondage. And only by His light can one overcome the darkness of the age.

And no matter how deep the darkness, the evil, or the odds, the light of God will be greater still. For God is far greater than the gods. And in God is the power to overcome the powers of the gods. And in His Spirit is the power to overcome the spirits of the age.

For in the days of the gods, one must never bow one's knee to any idol, any darkness, or any evil. In days of darkness the light must not waver or weaken but must grow stronger. And if the dark grows darker still, then the light must shine all the more brightly into it. And those who will not give up will, in the end, prevail.

The End of the Gods

The gods have returned. They have ascended the thrones of the modern world. They seek to make every knee bow down before them. But their kingdom is false, their authority illegitimate, and their days numbered.

Their kingdom will end. And those who have stood for the light, who have lived their lives by the light, and who have believed in, hoped for, and waited for the light, for them the Light will come, and in that Light they will arise and shine. To them will come the kingdom in which there is no more darkness, no more tears, no more sorrow, and no more death.

———————◆◆◆———————

The gods have returned. But their days will come to an end. And evil will give way to the good, falsehood to the truth, and the darkness to the breaking of dawn. Then the illusions of the night, its dreams and nightmares, will fade into the waking of the day, and the gods into the brightness of His coming, the coming of Him who is the only Light—and who alone is God.

Epilogue

IT IS NOW the day after the finishing of the book. There was to be no epilogue. But something happened on the day the book was completed to change that. And so I was asked to write something more.

The Return of the Gods was finished on June 24, 2022. Of all days on which to be completed, it was the day on which perhaps the most dramatic Supreme Court ruling in living memory was handed down. The court overturned Roe v. Wade, the ruling that made it illegal for abortion to be prohibited in any part of the nation.

My previous book, *The Harbinger II*, came out in 2020. In the chapter titled "The Plague" I wrote of the Jubilee of abortion. In the Bible the Jubilee was the year of restoration, restitution, redemption, release, freedom, reversing, and undoing. The Jubilee came once every fifty years.

Abortion on demand began in America in the year 1970. Prominent in pioneering abortion on demand was New York. It quickly became the nation's abortion capital. The prophet Jeremiah warned his nation that the shedding of its children's blood would lead to judgment. The death of the little ones would be answered by the death of the generation that had murdered them. One of the ways in which that death would come, according to Jeremiah's prophecy, would be in the form of a plague.

The fiftieth year after New York legalized abortion on demand came to its conclusion in 2020. It was the Jubilean year of abortion's entrance into America. That year death came to America as it had in ancient times, in the form of a plague. The plague was given the name COVID-19.

The connections between what happened in 2020, when the plague struck America, and what happened in 1970, when America began embracing abortion, and what happened in its wake, were stunning and eerie. Those connections, which I shared in *The Harbinger II*, involved correlations of places, times, and exact dates. In the year of Jubilee, if you took what did not belong to you, that which you took would be taken from you. America had taken life. Now, in the year of Jubilee, life would be taken from America.

But there was another year and another mystery. What began in 1970 culminated in 1973 when the Supreme Court ruled on Roe v. Wade and, in effect, made abortion the law of the land. That meant another Jubilee was coming. When was the Jubilean year of the Supreme Court ruling?

The fiftieth year began on January 22, 2022, and would last until January 22, 2023.

In *The Harbinger II*, I wrote this concerning the fiftieth year of abortion in America:

> The Jubilee was the reversal of what had been done since the last Jubilee.[1]

So in the Jubilean year of 2022, what had taken place in 1973, Roe v. Wade, was reversed. What had been done was undone. The Supreme Court of the fiftieth year had reversed and undone the ruling of the Supreme Court fifty years earlier.

The last of the three gods that make up the dark trinity is Molech. He was, as we have seen, the god especially known for child sacrifice and thus the principality most especially bound to and behind abortion. It was a striking thing that the last revisions needed for the book in the days leading up to the Supreme Court ruling focused on the sacrifices of the god Molech.

The ruling that overturned Roe v. Wade did not end abortion. It did not bring the reign of Molech to an end. But it did inaugurate a turning back. In many parts of the nation it would render his altars inoperable or remove them altogether.

There were times in ancient Israel's history that the nation was saved from the brink of judgment. It happened in the days of spiritual revival, when the nation turned back to God. The most salient sign of that revival and that turning back was the breaking down or removing of the altars that dotted the land in honor of the gods—specifically the altars of Baal and Molech.

In the wake of the Supreme Court decision of 2022, America would witness, in many of its regions, the removal and breaking of Molech's modern-day altars. Would it be a sign of revival, the beginning of a nation's return to God and its restoration? Or would it be an anomaly over which the nation will further divide as it continues its fall from God? If it is to be the second, then the future is judgment. If it is to be the first, then it must come through prayer, repentance, a true turning back, true change, and true spiritual revival. The changing of laws will, in the end, fail if there is not also the changing of hearts. And the changing of hearts comes from God and through revival.

The fact that *The Return of the Gods* was completed on the day that the

Supreme Court, after fifty years, overturned its ruling on abortion is significant. The book uncovers the gods and their works in our own day. The Supreme Court ruling was a turning back of Molech. It was an act of life against death. It was a stand against the gods, the breaking down of their altars.

And it was a sign to all those who seek to walk in the ways of God and who are called by His name to take encouragement, heart, strength, hope, and courage—and to live unbowed in the face of the gods. It is time to be strong and of good courage. It is time to be bold. It is time to let go of all fear and concern and to take a stand against the darkness and for the light.

The darkness will end, but the light will be forever. And so as it is written, be strong in the Lord and in the power of His might, for greater, much greater, is He who is in you than he who is in the world.

—JONATHAN CAHN

JUNE 25, 2022

Notes

Chapter 3

1. Deuteronomy 32:17, author's translation.
2. Psalm 106:36–37, author's translation.
3. Brenton Septuagint Translation, author's translation.
4. Author's translation.
5. 1 Corinthians 10:20, emphasis added, author's translation.

Chapter 5

1. Acts 16:16.
2. R. A. Tomlinson, "Delphi," Encyclopedia of Ancient Greece, ed. Nigel Wilson (New York: Routledge, 2006), 211, https://www.google.com/books/edition/Encyclopedia_of_Ancient_Greece/8pXhAQAAQBAJ?hl=en&gbpv=1.1

Chapter 6

1. Matthew 12:43–44.
2. Matthew 12:45.
3. Matthew 12:44.
4. Matthew 12:45.

Chapter 7

1. Ephesians 6:12.

Chapter 8

1. John Winthrop, "A Modell of Christian Charity," sermon, 1630, https://history.hanover.edu/texts/winthmod.html.

Chapter 9

1. Judges 2:11–12, emphasis added.
2. Eusebius, *Praeparatio Evangelica*, Book I, tr. E. H. Gifford, 1903, https://www.tertullian.org/fathers/eusebius_pe_01_book1.htm.

Chapter 10

1. "Pledge of Allegiance to the Flag; Manner of Delivery," United States Code, Title 4, chapter 1, section 4, 2018, https://www.govinfo.gov/content/pkg/USCODE-2018-title4/html/USCODE-2018-title4-chap1-sec4.htm.
2. Judges 3:7.
3. Jeremiah 23:27, KJV.
4. 2 Kings 17:15–16.
5. Exodus 20:3.
6. 2 Kings 17:16.

7. See, for example, Jon Meacham, "Meacham: The End of Christian America," *Newsweek*, April 3, 2009, https://www.newsweek.com/meacham-end-christian-america-77125; Norman Wirzba, "Why We Can Now Declare the End of 'Christian America,'" *Washington Post*, February 25, 2016, https://www.washingtonpost.com/news/acts-of-faith/wp/2016/02/25/why-we-can-now-declare-the-end-of-christian-america/.

Chapter 12

1. 2 Kings 17:16, emphasis added.
2. Wikipedia, s.v. "Charging Bull," modified April 16, 2022, https://en.wikipedia.org/wiki/Charging_Bull.
3. Dianne L. Durante, *Outdoor Monuments of Manhattan* (New York: NYU Press, 2007), chapter 5, https://www.google.com/books/edition/Outdoor_Monuments_of_Manhattan/1nMnB-2HgbwC?hl=en&gbpv=1.
4. George Washington, "Washington's Inaugural Address of 1789," National Archives, April 30, 1789, https://www.archives.gov/exhibits/american_originals/inaugtxt.html.
5. Winthrop, "A Modell of Christian Charity."

Chapter 14

1. Hosea 11:2.
2. Isaiah 2:8.
3. Acts 17:16.
4. Acts 17:29.
5. Psalm 115:4–5, 8, emphasis added.

Chapter 15

1. Guglielmo Mattioli, "ISIS-Destroyed Palmyra Arch Recreated in New York City," *Metropolis*, September 21, 2016, https://metropolismag.com/viewpoints/isis-destroyed-palmyra-arch-recreated-in-new-york-city/.

Chapter 16

1. Exodus 32:7, emphasis added.

Chapter 17

1. Eva Anagnostou-Laoutides and Michael B. Charles, "Herodotus on Sacred Marriage and Sacred Prostitution at Babylon," *Kernos* 31 (2018): 9–37, https://doi.org/10.4000/kernos.2653, emphasis added.

Chapter 18

1. Judges 2:13, emphasis added.
2. Judges 10:6, emphasis added.
3. 1 Samuel 12:10.

Chapter 20

1. Morris Silver, "Temple/Sacred Prostitution in Ancient Mesopotamia Revisited," PDFCoffee, accessed May 25, 2022, https://pdfcoffee.com/temple-sacred-prostitution-in-ancient-mesopotamia-revisited-pdf-free.html.
2. "Hymn to Inana as Ninegala (Inana D)," 95–106, Electronic Text Corpus of Sumerian Literature, accessed May 25, 2022, https://etcsl.orinst.ox.ac.uk/section4/tr4074.htm.
3. Rivkah Harris, "Inanna-Ishtar as Paradox and a Coincidence of Opposites," *History of Religions* 30, no. 3 (February 1991): 261–278, https://www.jstor.org/stable/1062957.
4. "Hymn to Inana as Ninegala (Inana D)," 109–115.
5. Melissa Hope Ditmore, ed., *Encyclopedia of Prostitution and Sex Work*, vol. 1 (Westport, CT: Greenwood Press, 2006), 35.
6. Harris, "Inanna-Ishtar as Paradox and a Coincidence of Opposites."

Chapter 21

1. Edward Kern, "Can It Happen Here?," *LIFE*, October 17, 1969, 77, https://books.google.com/books?id=JFAEAAAAMBAJ&pg.1

Chapter 22

1. 1 Kings 11:7.
2. Leviticus 18:21.
3. 2 Kings 23:10.
4. John Milton, *Paradise Lost*, I.392–396, https://www.paradiselost.org/8-search.html.
5. Winston Churchill, *The Gathering Storm* (Boston: Houghton Mifflin, 1948), 64.
6. Diodorus Siculus, *The Library of History*, accessed June 6, 2022, XX.14.6, https://penelope.uchicago.edu/Thayer/E/Roman/Texts/Diodorus_Siculus/20A*.html#3.
7. Jeremiah 32:35.

Chapter 23

1. Deuteronomy 1:31.
2. Psalm 127:3, NLT.
3. Psalm 139:13, 15–16.
4. Matthew 19:14.
5. Matthew 18:3–5.
6. Quoted in *A Dictionary of Early Christian Beliefs*, ed. David W. Bercot, s.v. "abortion, infanticide" (Peabody, Massachusetts: Hendrickson Publishers, 2013).
7. *A Dictionary of Early Christian Beliefs*, ed. David W. Bercot, s.v. "abortion, infanticide," emphasis added.

Chapter 25

1. Carrie Ann Murray, *Diversity of Sacrifice: Form and Function of Sacrificial Practices in the Ancient World and Beyond* (New York: State University of New York Press, 2017), 106.
2. Isaiah 49:15.

3. Plutarch, *Moralia, De Superstitione*, 13, ed. Frank Cole Babbitt, Perseus Digital Library, accessed June 6, 2022, https://www.perseus.tufts.edu/hopper/text?doc=Perseus%3Atext%3A2008.01.0189%3Asection%3D13.

4. Diodorus Siculus, *The Library of History*, XX.14.4.

5. Plutarch, *Moralia, De Superstitione*, 13.

6. Albert I. Baumgartner, *The Phoenician History of Philo of Byblos* (Leiden, Netherlands: Brill, 1981), 244.

7. Plato, *Minos*, 315b–315c, trans. W. R. M. Lamb, Perseus Digital Library, accessed June 6, 2022, http://www.perseus.tufts.edu/hopper/text?doc=Perseus%3Atext%3A1999.01.0180%3Atext%3DMinos%3Asection%3D315b, emphasis added.

8. Ginette Paris, *The Sacrament of Abortion*, trans. Joanna Mott (Washington, DC: Spring Publications, 1992), 92, emphasis added.

9. Sarah Terzo, "Clinic Owner: Abortion Is a Sacrament and Done for Love of the Baby," NRL News Today, April 27, 2016, https://www.nationalrighttolifenews.org/2016/04/clinic-owner-abortion-is-a-sacrament-and-done-for-love-of-the-baby/, emphasis added.

10. Paris, *The Sacrament of Abortion*, 56, emphasis added.

11. Ginette Paris, *The Psychology of Abortion*, 2nd ed., originally published as *The Sacrament of Abortion* (Washington, DC: Spring Publications, 2007), 70, emphasis added.

12. Paris, *The Sacrament of Abortion*, 8, emphasis added.

Chapter 26

1. Jeremiah 19:4, emphasis added.

2. Jeremiah 7:31.

Chapter 27

1. "A Shir-Namshub to Inana (Inana I)," A:16–22, Electronic Text Corpus of Sumerian Literature, accessed May 28, 2022, https://etcsl.orinst.ox.ac.uk/section4/tr4079.htm#:~:text=When%20I%20sit%20in%20the,the%20girlfriend%20of%20a%20woman.

2. Harris, "Inanna-Ishtar as Paradox and a Coincidence of Opposites."

3. "A Hymn to Inana for Išme-Dagan (Išme-Dagan K)," 19–31, Electronic Text Corpus of Sumerian Literature, accessed May 28, 2022, https://etcsl.orinst.ox.ac.uk/cgi-bin/etcsl.cgi?text=t.2.5.4.11#.1

Chapter 28

1. Joshua J. Mark, "Inanna," World History Encyclopedia, October 15, 2010, https://www.worldhistory.org/Inanna/.

2. "Inana and Ebiḫ," 1–6, Electronic Text Corpus of Sumerian Literature, accessed May 28, 2022, https://etcsl.orinst.ox.ac.uk/cgi-bin/etcsl.cgi?text=t.1.3.2#.

3. "A Hymn to Inana for Išme-Dagan (Išme-Dagan K)," 19–31, emphasis added.

4. Silver, "Temple/Sacred Prostitution in Ancient Mesopotamia Revisited," emphasis added.

5. Betsey Stevenson and Justin Wolfers, "The Paradox of Declining Female Happiness," Yale University, accessed May 26, 2022, https://law.yale.edu/sites/default/files/

documents/pdf/Intellectual_Life/Stevenson_ParadoxDecliningFemaleHappiness_
Dec08.pdf.

Chapter 29

1. Gina Konstantopoulos, "My Men Have Become Women, and My Women Men: Gender, Identity, and Cursing in Mesopotamia," *Die Welt des Orients* (2020): 363, https://doi.org/10.13109/wdor.2020.50.2.358.
2. "A Hymn to Inana for Išme-Dagan (Išme-Dagan K)," 19–31, emphasis added.
3. Konstantopoulos, "My Men Have Become Women."
4. Zainab Bahrani, *Women of Babylon: Gender and Representation in Mesopotamia* (London: Routledge, 2001), 159–160.

Chapter 30

1. Hazel Loveridge, "Inanna, Androgynous Queen of Heaven and Earth," Academia, accessed May 28, 2022, https://www.academia.edu/38150357/Inanna_Androgynous_Queen_of_Heaven_and_Earth.docx%20(25.01.%202019.
2. Loveridge, "Inanna, Androgynous Queen of Heaven and Earth."
3. Jake Thomas, "Disney Addresses Removal of 'Ladies and Gentlemen, Boys and Girls' in Video," *Newsweek*, March 29, 2022, https://www.newsweek.com/disney-remove-all-mentions-gender-roles-theme-parks-1693158.
4. "A Hymn to Inana for Išme-Dagan (Išme-Dagan K)," 19–31.

Chapter 31

1. Gordon H. Johnston, "Nahum's Rhetorical Allusions to Neo-Assyrian Treaty Curses," *Bibliotheca Sacra* 158 (October–December 2001): 415–436, https://www.academia.edu/39924918/Nahums_Rhetorical_Allusions_to_Neo_Assyrian_Treaty_Curses.
2. "A Hymn to Inana for Išme-Dagan," (Išme-Dagan K), 19–31, emphasis added.

Chapter 32

1. "A Hymn to Inana for Išme-Dagan," (Išme-Dagan K), 19–31, emphasis added.
2. Kelsie Ehalt, "Assumptions About the Assinnu: Gender, Sex, and Sexuality in Ancient Texts and Modern Scholarship" (master's thesis, Brandeis University, 2021), 19, https://scholarworks.brandeis.edu/view/delivery/01BRAND_INST/1243832752000
1921/13438327510001921, emphasis added.
3. Nadav Na'aman, "The Ishtar Temple at Alalakh," *Journal of Near Eastern Studies* 39 (1980): 209–214, http://www.jstor.org/stable/544242.
4. "A Shir-Namshub to Inana (Inana I)," A:16–22.
5. Ciaran McGrath, "Investigation as Number of Girls Seeking Gender Transition Treatment Rises 4,515 Percent," *Express*, updated September 16, 2018, https://www.express.co.uk/news/uk/1018407/gender-transition-treatment-investigation-penny-mordaunt.

Chapter 34

1. Emma Lazarus, "The New Colussus," National Park Service, November 2, 1883, https://www.nps.gov/stli/learn/historyculture/colossus.htm.
2. "Inana and Mt. Ebih," The Ishtar Gate, accessed May 30, 2022, https://www.theishtargate.com/inana-ebih.html.
3. "The Descent of Ishtar," *Sources for the History of Western Civilization*, ed. Michael Burger, 2nd edition (Toronto: University of Toronto Press, 2015).

Chapter 35

1. Julia Assante, "Sex, Magic and the Liminal Body in the Erotic Art and Texts of the Old Babylonian Period," *Sex and Gender in the Ancient Near East*, eds. Simo Parpola and Robert M. Whiting (2002): 27–52, https://www.academia.edu/1817695/_Sex_Magic_and_the_Liminal_Body_in_the_Erotic_Art_and_Texts_of_the_Old_Babylonian_Period_Sex_and_Gender_in_the_Ancient_Near_East_Actes_de_la_XLVIIe_Rencontre_Assyriologique_Internationale_Helsinki_2_6_July_2001_Simo_Parpola_and_Robert_M_Whiting_eds_Helsinki_2002_27_51.
2. Assante, "Sex, Magic and the Liminal Body in the Erotic Art and Texts of the Old Babylonian Period."
3. "A Shir-Namshub to Inana (Inana I)," A:16–22, emphasis added.
4. Samuel Noah Kramer, *The Sacred Marriage Rite: Aspects of Faith, Myth, and Ritual in Ancient Sumer* (Bloomington, IN: Indiana University Press, 1969), 132.
5. Thorkild Jacobsen, "Pictures and Pictorial Language (The Burney Relief)," *Figurative Language in the Ancient Near East*, eds. M. Mindlin, M. J. Geller, and J. E. Wansbrough (London: Taylor & Francis, 2005), 5.
6. Richard A. Henshaw, *Female and Male: The Cultic Personnel: The Bible and the Rest of the Ancient Near East* (Eugene, OR: Pickwick Publications, 1994), 313; "Inana and Enki," Segment I, 41–46, Electronic Text Corpus of Sumerian Literature, accessed May 28, 2022, https://etcsl.orinst.ox.ac.uk/cgi-bin/etcsl.cgi?text=t.1.3.1#; Loveridge, "Inanna, Androgynous Queen of Heaven and Earth."

Chapter 36

1. "Inana and Enki," A:41–46, Electronic Text Corpus of Sumerian Literature, accessed June 11, 2022, https://etcsl.orinst.ox.ac.uk/cgi-bin/etcsl.cgi?text=t.1.3.1#.
2. "A Shir-Namshub to Inana (Inana I)," A:16–22.
3. "A Šir-Namursaĝa to Ninsiana for Iddin-Dagan (Iddin-Dagan A)," 45–58, Electronic Text Corpus of Sumerian Literature, accessed May 28, 2022, https://etcsl.orinst.ox.ac.uk/cgi-bin/etcsl.cgi?text=t.2.5.3.1#.

Chapter 37

1. *Epic of Gilgamesh*, Internet Archive, accessed May 29, 2022, https://archive.org/stream/TheEpicofGilgamesh_201606/eog_djvu.txt.
2. *Epic of Gilgamesh*, trans. Maureen Gallery Kovacs, Ancient Texts, accessed May 28, 2022, http://www.ancienttexts.org/library/mesopotamian/gilgamesh/tab6.htm.
3. *Epic of Gilgamesh*, trans. Maureen Gallery Kovacs, emphasis added.

Chapter 38

1. "Hymn to Inana as Ninegala (Inana D)," 1–8.
2. Ronald M. Glassman, *The Origins of Democracy in Tribes, City-States and Nation-States*, vol. 1 (New York: Springer, 2017), 337.
3. "Inana and Ebih," 7–9, Electronic Text Corpus of Sumerian Literature, accessed May 28, 2022, https://etcsl.orinst.ox.ac.uk/section1/tr132.htm.
4. Jeremy A. Black, ed., *The Literature of Ancient Sumer* (Oxford, UK: Oxford University Press, 2006), 94.
5. Quoted in Theodore J. Lewis, "CT 13.33-34 AND EZEKIEL 32: LION-DRAGON MYTHS," Academia, accessed May 30, 2022, https://www.academia.edu/21870790/_CT_13.33-34_and_Ezekiel_32_Lion-Dragon_Myths_Journal_of_the_American_Oriental_Society_116_1996_28-47.

Chapter 39

1. "Descent of the Goddess Ishtar Into the Lower World," Sacred Texts, accessed May 30, 2022, https://www.sacred-texts.com/ane/ishtar.htm.
2. David Carter, *Stonewall: The Riots That Sparked the Gay Revolution* (New York: St. Martin's Press, 2004), 151.
3. "The Descent of Ishtar," Columbia University, accessed May 31, 2022, http://www.columbia.edu/itc/religion/f2001/edit/docs/ishtar.htm.
4. "Inana's Descent to the Nethre World," Electronic Text Corpus of Sumerian Literature, accessed May 28, 2022, https://etcsl.orinst.ox.ac.uk/section1/tr141.htm, 295–305.
5. "The Exaltation of Inana (Inana B)," Electronic Text Corpus of Sumerian Literature, accessed May 28, 2022, https://etcsl.orinst.ox.ac.uk/section4/tr4072.htm, 20–33.
6. "Inana and Ebih," 131–137.
7. "Inana and Ebih," 1–6.
8. James B. Pritchard, *The Ancient Near East: An Anthology of Texts and Pictures* (Princeton, NJ: Princeton University Press, 2021), 334.
9. Diane Wolkstein and Samuel Noah Kramer, *Inanna: Queen of Heaven and Earth* (New York: Harper & Row, 1983), 95.

Chapter 40

1. Benjamin Read Foster, *Before the Muses: An Anthology of Akkadian Literature* (Bethesda, MD: CDL Press, 2005), 601–603.
2. *Epic of Gilgamesh*, trans. Kovacs.
3. Stephanie Budin, *The Myth of Sacred Prostitution in Antiquity* (Cambridge, UK: Cambridge University Press, 2008).
4. Marten Stol, *Women in the Ancient Near East* (Boston: DeGruyter, 2016), 21.2.
5. Norman Yoffee, *Myths of the Archaic State* (Cambridge, UK: Cambridge University Press, 2004), 125.
6. *Epic of Gilgamesh*, trans. N. K. Sanders, Maricopa Community College, accessed May 31, 2022, https://open.maricopa.edu/worldmythologyvolume2heroicmythology/chapter/the-epic-of-gilgamesh/.

7. Donn Teal, *The Gay Militants* (New York: St. Martin's Press, 1971), 21.

8. Donn Teal, *The Gay Militants*.

9. Stephanie Dalley, *Myths From Mesopotamia* (Oxford, UK: Oxford University Press, 1989), 155.

10. "The Exaltation of Inana (Inana B)," 13–19.

11. Carter, *Stonewall*, 175.

Chapter 41

1. S. Langdon, *Tammuz and Ishtar* (Oxford, UK: Oxford University Press, 1914), 176.

2. Vladimir Emeliav, "Cultic Calendar and Psychology of Time: Elements of Common Semantics in Explanatory and Astrological Texts of Ancient Mesopotamia," *Comparative Mythology* 5, no. 1 (December 2019): 22, https://www.academia.edu/41435826/Cultic_Calendar_and_Psychology_of_Time_Elements_of_Common_Semantics_in_Explanatory_and_Astrological_Texts_of_Ancient_Mesopotamia.

Chapter 42

1. Wolkstein and Kramer, *Inanna*, 97.

Chapter 43

1. Wolkstein and Kramer, *Inanna*, 97.

2. Wolkstein and Kramer, *Inanna*, 99.

3. Cheryl Morgan, "Evidence for Trans Lives in Sumer," *Notches* (blog), May 2, 2017, https://notchesblog.com/2017/05/02/evidence-for-trans-lives-in-sumer/.

4. Gordon J. Wenham, "The Old Testament Attitude to Homosexuality," *Expository Times* 102, no. 9 (1991): 259–263, https://biblicalstudies.org.uk/article_attitude_wenham.html.

5. Wolkstein and Kramer, *Inanna*, 97.

6. "Ancient Babylon," Let There Be Light Ministries, accessed May 31, 2022, http://www.lightministries.com/id955.htm.

7. Gwendolyn Leick, ed., *The Babylonian World* (New York: Routledge, 2007).

8. Leick, *The Babylonian World*.

9. "A Hymn to Inana (Inana C)," 1–10, 73–79, Electronic Text Corpus of Sumerian Literature, accessed May 28, 2022, https://etcsl.orinst.ox.ac.uk/cgi-bin/etcsl.cgi?text=t.4.07.3#, emphasis added.

10. Géza G. Xeravits, ed., *Religion and Female Body in Ancient Judaism and Its Environments* (Berlin: DeGruyter, 2015), 18.

Chapter 44

1. Sappho, "Ode to Aphrodite," All Poetry, accessed May 31, 2022, https://allpoetry.com/poem/14327741-Ode-To-Aphrodite-by-Sappho.

2. Hugh G. Evelyn-White, "Hymn 6 to Aphrodite," Tufts University, 1914, https://www.perseus.tufts.edu/hopper/text?doc=Perseus%3Atext%3A1999.01.0138%3Ahymn%3D6%3Acard%3D1.

3. Wolkstein and Kramer, *Inanna*, 99.

4. Wolkstein and Kramer, *Inanna*, 99.

5. Wolkstein and Kramer, *Inanna*, 99.

Chapter 45

1. *Jamieson, Fausset, and Brown Commentary on the Whole Bible, Deluxe Edition*, s.v. "Tammuz" (Harrington, DE: Delmarva, 2013), emphasis added.

2. Joseph Benson, *Commentary on the Old and New Testaments*, "Ezekiel 8:14," Bible Comments, accessed May 31, 2022, https://www.biblecomments.org/c/1/joseph-bensons-commentary-on-the-old-and-new-testaments/ezekiel/8/14.

3. Hieronymus, Commentarii, in *Ezechielem*, III.8.36, Monumenta, accessed May 31, 2022, http://www.monumenta.ch/latein/text.php?tabelle=Hieronymus&rumpfid=Hieronymus,%20Commentarii,%20in%20Ezechielem,%2003,%2008&level=5&domain=&lang=1&id=&hilite_id=&links=&inframe=1&hide_apparatus=1, emphasis added.

4. Hieronymus, Commentarii, in *Ezechielem*, III.8.36, emphasis added.

5. International Standard Bible Encyclopedia Online, "Tammuz," accessed May 31, 2022, https://www.internationalstandardbible.com/T/tammuz.html.

6. Lucian, *The Syrian Goddess* (n.p.: Phoemixx Classics Ebooks, 2021), https://www.google.com/books/edition/The_Syrian_Goddess/YsRTEAAAQBAJ?hl=en&gbpv=0.

7. Eusebius, "Chapter LV.—Overthrow of an Idol Temple, and Abolition of Licentious Practices, at Aphaca in Phœnicia," Christian Classics Ethereal Library, accessed May 31, 2022, https://www.ccel.org/ccel/schaff/npnf201.iv.vi.iii.lv.html.

8. Socrates Scholasticus, "Chapter XVIII.—The Emperor Constantine Abolishes Paganism and Erects Many Churches in Different Places," Christian Classics Ethereal Library, accessed May 31, 2022, https://www.ccel.org/ccel/schaff/npnf202.ii.iv.xviii.html.

Chapter 46

1. S. G. F. Brandon, *Man and His Destiny in the Great Religions* (Manchester, UK: Manchester University Press, 1962), 102.

2. "To Ishtar," Cuneiform Digital Library Initiative, accessed May 31, 2022, https://cdli.ox.ac.uk/wiki/doku.php?id=to_ishtar.

3. Wolkstein and Kramer, *Inanna*, 95.

4. *Epic of Gilgamesh*, trans. N. K. Sanders.

5. "To Ishtar," Cuneiform Digital Library Initiative.

6. "Inana and Shu-kale-tuda," 239–255, Electronic Text Corpus of Sumerian Literature, accessed May 28, 2022, https://etcsl.orinst.ox.ac.uk/section1/tr133.htm, emphasis added.

Chapter 47

1. Langdon, *Tammuz and Ishtar*, 167, emphasis added.

2. Emeliav, "Cultic Calendar and Psychology of Time."

Chapter 48

1. "Inana and Shu-kale-tuda," 239–255, emphasis added.

Chapter 49

1. "A Hymn to Inana (Inana C)," 18–28.

Chapter 50

1. "The Baal Epic," Hanover College, accessed May 31, 2022, https://history.hanover.edu/courses/excerpts/260baal.html.
2. "Inana and Ebih," 25–36.

Chapter 52

1. Ephesians 2:12.
2. Exodus 15:11.
3. John 14:6, emphasis added.
4. Matthew 11:28, emphasis added.

Epilogue

1. Jonathan Cahn, *The Harbinger II* (Lake Mary, FL: FrontLine, 2020), 228.

About Jonathan Cahn

Jonathan Cahn caused a worldwide stir with the release of the *New York Times* best seller *The Harbinger* and his subsequent *New York Times* best sellers. He has addressed members of Congress and spoken at the United Nations. He was named, along with Billy Graham and Keith Green, one of the top forty spiritual leaders of the last forty years "who radically changed our world." He is known as a prophetic voice to our times and for the opening up of the deep mysteries of God. Jonathan leads Hope of the World, a ministry of getting the Word to the world and sponsoring projects of compassion to the world's most needy; and Beth Israel/the Jerusalem Center, his ministry base and worship center in Wayne, New Jersey, just outside New York City. He is a much-sought-after speaker and appears throughout America and the world.

To get in touch, to receive prophetic updates, to receive free gifts from his ministry (special messages and much more), to find out about his over two thousand messages and mysteries, for more information, to contact him, or to have a part in the Great Commission, use the following contacts.

Check out:	**Write direct to:**
HopeoftheWorld.org	Hope of the World
	Box 1111
	Lodi, NJ 07644 USA

To be kept up to date and see what's happening:

Facebook:	Jonathan Cahn (official site)
YouTube:	Jonathan Cahn
Twitter:	@Jonathan_Cahn
Instagram:	jonathan.cahn
Email:	contact@hopeoftheworld.org

To find out how you can go to the Holy Land with Jonathan on one of his upcoming Israel Super Tours, write to: contact@hopeoftheworld.org or check online for the coming Super Tours.

Our FREE GIFT to You

Dear Reader,

We hope you found *The Return of the Gods* to be as explosive as all of Jonathan Cahn's other books.

If you aren't aware of how it all started and would like to learn more about what caused a worldwide sensation, we have a **FREE GIFT** for you.

Link to stream
The Harbinger Decoded online
(video run time: 62 minutes)

Scan the code above
to get this **FREE GIFT**, or go to:

www.booksbyjonathancahn.com/freemovie

Thanks again, and God bless you,

Publisher of FrontLine books

FRONT
LINE